THE ESSENTIAL GUIDEBOOK TO
MINDFULNESS IN RECOVERY

The Essential Guidebook to
MINDFULNESS
in RECOVERY

JOHN BRUNA

CENTRAL RECOVERY PRESS

LAS VEGAS

Central Recovery Press (CRP) is committed to publishing exceptional materials addressing addiction treatment, recovery, and behavioral healthcare topics.

For more information, visit www.centralrecoverypress.com.

Publisher: Central Recovery Press
               3321 N. Buffalo Drive
               Las Vegas, NV 89129

23 22 21 20 19 18   1 2 3 4 5

ISBN: 978-1-942094-85-2 (print)
      978-1-942094-86-9 (e-book))

Photo of John Bruna by Jeffrey S. Rose. Used with permission.

Every attempt has been made to contact copyright holders. If copyright holders have not been properly acknowledged, please contact us. Central Recovery Press will be happy to rectify the omission in future printings of this book.

Publisher's Note: This book contains general information about mindfulness, addiction recovery, and related matters. The information is not medical advice. This book is not an alternative to medical advice from your doctor or other professional healthcare provider.

Our books represent the experiences and opinions of their authors only. Every effort has been made to ensure that events, institutions, and statistics presented in our books as facts are accurate and up-to-date. To protect their privacy, the names of some of the people, places, and institutions in this book may have been changed.

Cover and interior design and layout by Sara Streifel, Think Creative Design.

Like ripples on a pond, our kindness can spread and flow.
We can be a voice of compassion and unity,
skillfully recognizing the value of all.
We can all help improve the world,
one mindful smile and compassionate activity at a time.

John Bruna, *The Wisdom of a Meaningful Life*

TABLE OF CONTENTS

Introduction..ix

What Is Mindfulness?.. 1

Meditation.. 9

Values.. 15

Attention 39

Wisdom.. 61

Equanimity.. 81

Compassion.. 107

Loving-Kindness.. 137

Action 163

More Wisdom.. 189

Mindfulness Skills Summary and Review............. 213

Continuing the Practice..................................... 235

About Mindfulness in Recovery.......................... 237

Values List.. 238

Daily Morning Reflections 240

INTRODUCTION

Whether or not it feels like it right now, you are incredibly fortunate. You have all the resources available to improve your life and become the person you really want to be. The fact that you're reading this guidebook means that all the conditions of your life—including the hardships and struggles—have provided you with the precious opportunity to find recovery and rediscover your worthiness and value as a human being.

All of us who have struggled with our addiction know well the deep emotional and mental pain it has caused ourselves and others. We know what it is like to be completely powerless over our impulses and cravings, consistently acting on them regardless of the consequences. We know well the deep shame we feel as a result of our actions. What we have been unaware of is that we can change. We do not need to be prisoners of our thoughts, emotions, habits, impulses, or cravings. There is no need for us to continue to engage in activities that rob us of our self-worth and dignity.

We can learn skills that allow us to be the people we want to be—people of integrity, capable of engaging in activities that are in alignment with our deepest values and living lives that are truly meaningful. Instead of being prisoners of unhealthy habits, we can consciously create healthy ones that support our recovery and the lives we want to live.

Throughout our lives, we have all learned to do many things to survive. We have been taught to walk, speak, read, and write and have developed many skills through practice and with the guidance of others. However, few of us have ever been taught how to train our minds. Without training, our minds can easily get caught up in every fear, worry, desire, or impulse that arises.

Rather than being a prisoner of the thoughts and emotions you experience, you can learn to be more mindful, able to consciously respond to thoughts, impulses, and emotions with more choice and freedom. Just like any other skill, all it takes is training and practice. Science has demonstrated that you can literally rewire yourself, creating new neuropathways in your brain. You can do this on purpose, consciously developing healthy habits and attitudes that support the life you want to live.

The Essential Guidebook to Mindfulness in Recovery is designed to help you develop the specific skills that empower you to succeed. You really can change, find freedom, and live the life you find most meaningful! If you are in treatment, you are in a safe and supportive environment, surrounded by highly trained and caring people whose primary concern is to help you develop the inner resources that will allow you to fully engage in your life of recovery. Few people will ever have the opportunity that you have now, so I strongly encourage you to take full advantage of it and start becoming the person you want to be today.

If you are not in treatment and are new to recovery, surround yourself with as many supportive and healthy people as possible and seize this precious opportunity to transform your life. If you have already found recovery and are inspired to tackle problems limiting your full development, this guidebook will be an invaluable resource for you to discover genuine happiness and cultivate tools that will empower you to engage more productively in your life.

WHAT IS MINDFULNESS?

"Mindfulness is much more than present-moment awareness.
Mindfulness includes and facilitates the cultivation of
concentration, wisdom, and the ability to make healthy choices
that foster genuine happiness and a meaningful life."

JOHN BRUNA

What is it that prevents us from being the people we want to be? All of us are capable of making a list of things that we can do to improve our lives. Creating such a list is not difficult and would not even take much time; however, few people, whether they struggle with addiction or not, can actually consistently do the things on their list. Why is this the case?

If we can make a list of actions and values that we know would improve the quality of our lives, why is it so difficult to live by them? While there can be many reasons, one of the most common and powerful is simply that we are not even aware of what we are doing throughout much of our lives. Our minds are constantly distracted, going from one thought to another, ruminating about past or future events, and caught up in desire, worries, or concerns—all while we are doing other things, such as driving, working, or even trying to listen to a friend. This is why we often do not know where our car keys are even though we put them down just moments ago. Our minds were somewhere else when we set them down. How can we possibly make conscious, healthy choices if we are not even present to make them?

Our distracted and unruly minds are at the root of our problem. We have very little conscious control of our attention. If we are to establish any choice in our lives, we need to be able to direct our attention where we would like it to go rather than have our unruly mind dictate what we think about.

The first step in learning to live more mindfully is to develop our attention so that we can be more attentive and present in our own life. Once we are present in our life, we will have more opportunity to make the healthy choices that support the values of the life we want to live.

When beginning our journey in recovery, we are powerless over our thoughts, feelings, impulses, and habits. Our lives have become unmanageable, and we have become prisoners of our addictive thinking and habits. Despite our best intentions and honest desire to be good people, we find ourselves engaging in activities that we are ashamed of and consistently wind up harming ourselves and others.

As mentioned in the introduction, you do not need to be a prisoner of your addiction, thoughts, feelings, or habits. You can develop the ability to become aware of the harmful and unhealthy thoughts and habits that rob you of your ability to be the person you want to be and liberate yourself from them. You can develop the skill of attention, becoming aware of your thoughts instead of being dominated by them. In doing so, you can ultimately learn to choose one thought over another.

This brings us to step two, recognizing the insanity and suffering of chasing momentary pleasure at the expense of long-term happiness and basic dignity. Our sense of self-worth and dignity comes from living in alignment with our deepest values. How is it that we continually act in ways that are contrary to these values? If we want to feel good about ourselves, why do we do so many things that we don't feel good about? We do not need to be bound to these irrational and harmful behaviors. We can discover how to act in ways that honor our deepest values and we can be restored to sanity.

To return to sanity—that is, having our actions and behaviors reflect our personal values—we need to know what our values are and be able to bear them in mind as we engage in our lives, which is why it is important to take the time to reflect upon the values we find most meaningful. When was the last time you reflected upon your deepest values and asked yourself what a meaningful and fulfilling life is to you? How can you act upon your values if you don't know what they are?

In step three, we develop wisdom, a deep and clear realization that our self-centered and unrealistic view of the world is the real cause of much of our suffering. Though we can know the world only through our personal experience of it, we are not the center of the universe. There are powers greater than ourselves and our desires at play in the world. As obvious as it is that we are not the center of the universe, we constantly fall into the trap of believing that things should go the way we think they should.

The world was not created simply to fulfill our desires, meet our needs, and make us happy. Such misperceptions easily lead to feeling like a victim and thinking life is somehow unfair to us. Usually our greatest suffering does not come from the unpleasant things that happen in our lives; it comes from our belief that such things should not happen to us.

In truth, life is messy for all of us. No one is immune from the normal problems that arise in life on Earth. At the time of writing this guidebook, there are more than seven billion human beings on the planet. All of them are seeking happiness, experiencing struggles and hardships, have known sadness and despair, and are trying to get their needs met—just like you. You are part of the universe and, just like everyone else, you are subject to all the challenges and joys it brings. Realizing this can eliminate much suffering and empower you to respond—rather than react—to the ups and downs that will naturally come your way.

To be the person you want to be, it is necessary to know who that person is and bear in mind the qualities of that person as you engage in your life consciously, with attention and intention. As obvious as this seems, the skills required, as well as the habits you can cultivate to support you in the process, are rarely taught.

The Seven Skills of Living Mindfully in Recovery

As you engage in your recovery, this guidebook will help you cultivate and refine seven specific skills of living mindfully that will support your recovery and empower you to live your life in the ways you find most meaningful.

Values: Living a life of integrity, in alignment with your values, creates inner peace, well-being, and a meaningful life that supports your recovery. The Values section of this guidebook will help you identify and clarify your personal values and explore ways in which you can bring them into your daily activities. This skill helps you return to sanity, living in alignment with your values instead of acting in ways that fundamentally go against them.

Attention: Attentional balance is the focus of this skill. Using meditation to train your mind to be present and develop the ability to direct your attention where you choose—instead of constantly having it drawn away by thoughts, distractions, worries, or desires—helps you directly address feelings of powerlessness and unmanageability.

Wisdom: Develop insight into the realities of life and learn how to engage productively and realistically with the challenges it brings. In so doing, you recognize and nurture the healthy and wise choices that support your recovery as well as acknowledging and letting go of the unhealthy ones. Ultimately, the goal is to gain wisdom, not simply acquire knowledge. With wisdom, you are able let go of your afflicted and addicted sense of self-will and develop your higher self—a higher self that is healthy and connected to your values and spiritual path, as well as this precious thing we call life, in realistic and meaningful ways.

Equanimity: The skill of equanimity is often described as a mind of calm or composure. It is a balanced state of mind that is not caught up in extremes and allows you to be present and stable even in difficult and challenging situations. With equanimity, you are able to respond more quickly and skillfully to difficulties when they arise, seeing them as opportunities to grow. You are also able to more fully appreciate all the wonderful people and events that come your way.

Compassion: The wisdom of compassion is the ability to make healthy choices and engage in actions that remove or reduce suffering in yourself and others. It is out of compassion for yourself and others that you can find the inner strength to overcome your addiction and the harmful habits that have wreaked havoc in your life.

Loving-Kindness: The attitude of loving-kindness is the deep and sincere wish for yourself and others to be genuinely happy. In cultivating loving-kindness, or sincere friendliness as it is also called, you are supporting your recovery by developing the direct antidote to the destructive mental and emotional states of anger, hatred, and resentment.

Action: There is an old piece of wisdom that says you cannot think yourself into right living, but you can live yourself into right thinking. By putting mindfulness into action, you practice intentional living in ways that will create new neuropathways in your brain and healthy habits that support your recovery.

A New Beginning

"The only thing that separates the person you are from
the person you want to be is the action you take."

JOHN BRUNA

Right now, you have the opportunity, the resources, and a supportive environment to transform your life. You no longer need to be a prisoner of your addiction, habits, fears, or insecurities. In this guidebook, you will find tools to help you realize your personal freedom from bondage, discover your worthiness and value as a human being, and engage in a life you find meaningful—in essence, to become the person you want to be, a person capable of living a life in alignment with your deepest values.

The obvious starting point is taking some time to reflect upon your values and identify the ones that mean the most to you. Look at the values list in the Appendix, choose six values, and explain why they are currently important to you. You may have more than six, but the goal of this exercise is to get you thinking about and prioritizing them.

1. _____

   _____

   _____

2. _____

   _____

   _____

3. _____

   _____

   _____

4. _____

   _____

   _____

5. _____

   _____

   _____

6. _____

   _____

   _____

For each of your values, give an example of when you lived up to that value and how you felt about yourself as a result.

1. _____

_____

2. _____

_____

3. _____

_____

4. _____

_____

5. _____

_____

6. _____

_____

What do you think your life would be like if you were able to embody these values most of the time?

_____

_____

_____

_____

_____

_____

Knowing that today is the first day of the rest of your life and you have a new beginning with support to help you, write a clear description of the person you want to be. Be specific about the inner qualities, character, and attributes you want to grow. Do not write about outer goals, such as a career.

_____

_____

_____

_____

_____

_____

As you engage in your recovery, the goal is to help you develop mindfulness skills so you can enhance and grow the qualities and attributes that you listed as you become the person you aspire to be. This is your opportunity. All it takes is a consistent effort to do your best.

The key is establishing a good foundation and routine that allows you to bring recovery into your daily life in ways that are truly meaningful to you. Using the contents found in these pages as a guide will help you create such a practice.

A Spiritual Path

As mentioned earlier, *The Essential Guidebook to Mindfulness in Recovery* was designed to support members of all faiths and spiritual traditions, as well as those without a spiritual tradition. If you have a spiritual or religious path that is meaningful to you, it is very important that you integrate it as much as possible into your daily practices. If prayer is meaningful and important to you, make prayer a part of your daily practice.

If you do not have a spiritual or religious path, explore the question of what brings meaning and purpose to your life through a deep investigation of your personal values. It can be extremely helpful to your recovery to have a curious and discerning mind about what brings meaning to life and your role in it. If you find particular philosophies or spiritual principles that speak to you, explore them.

A Few Thoughts on Prayer

For some, prayer it is a religious practice. For others, prayer is a spiritual endeavor not directly related to any formal religion. Many people find comfort in memorizing and reciting prayers, and others feel it is important to pray spontaneously from the heart.

If your prayer comes from a motivation to improve yourself and the world in which we live—increasing harmony, understanding, love, and compassion—then regardless of the methods, words, or religion, prayer can be extremely beneficial.

Prayer does not need to be limited to a formal practice or religion. Wishing others well or sending them love can be your prayer. You may also find that your deepest prayers are sometimes without words, found when you quiet your mind in meditation.

Explore what prayer means to you; it can be as simple as cultivating good thoughts and aspirations for yourself and others. Here are a few quotes on prayer from various traditions that you may find beneficial during your reflection.

"Prayer is not asking. Prayer is putting oneself in the hands of God, at His disposition, and listening to His voice in the depth of our hearts."

MOTHER TERESA

"Prayer is not asking. It is a longing of the soul. It is daily admission of one's weakness. It is better in prayer to have a heart without words than words without a heart."

MAHATMA GANDHI

"The function of prayer is not to influence God, but rather to change the nature of the one who prays."

SOREN KIERKEGAARD

"The fewer the words, the better the prayer."

MARTIN LUTHER

"Prayer is an act of love; words are not needed. Even if sickness distracts from thoughts, all that is needed is the will to love."

SAINT TERESA OF AVILA

"The simplest acts of kindness are by far more powerful than a thousand heads bowing in prayer."

MAHATMA GANDHI

MEDITATION

Step One: Powerlessness and Unmanageability

The starting point for developing mindfulness is training your mind to focus on what you choose to focus on. You do not need to be powerless over your thoughts, feelings, and desires. You can start cultivating the ability to consciously choose one thought over another. The most effective method to train your mind is a consistent meditation practice.

Meditation allows you to focus your attention consciously. Much of the time we are distracted as our minds are constantly pulling our attention away to every thought, impulse, worry, desire, and fear that arises. We all know how powerless we can be over unhealthy thoughts and ruminations—what it feels like to be caught up in a resentment, a fear, or a desire and unable to let go.

As mentioned earlier, you can learn to let go of unhealthy thoughts, feel and respond to emotions instead of being a prisoner of them, and foster healthy attitudes that are based in reality instead of on the stories that can dominate your mind. The first step is to train the mind to attend to what you choose to attend to. The more you can consciously take charge of your attention and the thoughts you choose to engage in the more ability you will have to make healthy choices in your life.

There are many types of meditation, each designed with a specific purpose; however, your primary meditation will be a *shamatha* practice, as it is the most effective and efficient one to train and develop attention. Shamatha is a concentration practice that is specifically designed to cultivate attentional balance.

In shamatha meditation, you focus all your attention on one object to the exclusion of everything else. No matter what else arises—whether it be delicious thoughts, blissful feelings, or an itch—you maintain your attention on the chosen object of your meditation. As with any skill, if you practice this consistently, over time you will get better at it, increasing your concentration and the ability to direct your attention.

This meditation practice is also healthy for your body. It allows you to rest your body and mind in their natural states, which is healing. A bonus is that shamatha is a simple and straightforward practice that anyone can learn. It has three stages of development: relaxation, stability, and vividness. It is often explained using a tree as a metaphor.

The roots of the tree represent relaxation. For you to truly progress in this practice, you need to be able to relax the body while keeping the mind alert. As simple as this sounds, it is not easy and is a skill to be cultivated. In your busy and stressful life, your body is rarely physically relaxed while the mind is clear and mentally alert. You will notice that when you do relax, you usually have a tendency to feel tired and might even fall asleep. Most of the time, the nervous system is quite active and ramped up. Therefore, initially, your practice is simply learning how to relax your body without falling asleep.

As you develop your practice and learn to be alert while relaxed, what will become the trunk of your tree—stability—begins to sprout. Stability occurs when you can maintain your attention on your chosen object of meditation. If you have a consistent practice, even if it is only for a short time daily, you will learn to have a relaxed body and an alert mind that is eventually able to remain focused on what you have chosen to attend to for brief moments. This is a gradual process; trying to rush does not help.

At first, the mind will wander, and wander again, many times, challenging you to maintain stability. At this point, many people struggle and begin to believe that they are not capable of meditating. However, this is when you are actually making progress! If the mind wanders 1,000 times during meditation and you simply bring it back 1,000 times, that means you have just had 1,000 mindful moments that you would not have had otherwise. Every time you notice that your mind has wandered, you are being mindful, aware of where your attention is and able to direct it back consciously. This is the process of training the mind.

Most of the time, when the mind wanders, you are not aware of it; it just takes you along for the ride. However, gradually, with consistent practice, the trunk of stability will develop, and you will be able to rest your awareness on your chosen object for longer amounts of time.

Eventually, this will lead to a high degree of clarity and vividness in what you attend to, which forms the leaves of your tree. There is a sequence of development with this meditation practice: first relaxation, then stability, and finally vividness. Of course, in our goal-oriented modern Western world, people often try to reach for the leaves first, before they have developed healthy roots and a strong trunk. Rather than being beneficial, this hinders your progress. Patience and consistent practice, without attachment to a goal, will be much more productive.

As you increase your ability to focus and direct your attention, you will find that you are present, your memory will improve, and you will no longer be powerless over every thought, impulse, or fear that arises.

KEY POINT TO REMEMBER

We do not evaluate our meditation sessions by how focused or distracted we are.

We evaluate our meditation sessions by whether we are following the directions

and doing the practice properly. Like any other skill, such as learning to play an

instrument, it takes time and practice to improve.

As you practice, it is important to be consistent and not do too much too soon. Start with shorter sessions and increase them over time. You can find guided meditations of various lengths of time to assist you at www.mindfulnessinrecovery.org.

Begin with the morning recovery meditation that combines shamatha with a motivation to start your day. In the evening, try the "Transforming Unskillful Events" meditation for ten minutes to improve upon any actions you did not feel good about during the day.

As you finish the exercises in this guidebook and establish a stable meditation practice, you can explore different types of meditation available online in the Mindfulness in Recovery Community to meet your specific needs and enhance your practice.

Establishing a Daily Practice

One of the keys to establishing a successful daily morning practice is to start the evening before. Instead of waiting until you wake up to set an intention for the day, dedicate some time for reflection and/or meditation before you go to bed at night. You will find that this is extremely helpful the next morning, as you have already laid the groundwork before waking.

1. Upon awakening, as soon as possible, start shaping your motivation by calling to mind that you have the opportunity to wake up to another day in recovery. Bring this to mind quickly as a reminder of just how fortunate you truly are and to set the intention to use this day as an opportunity to develop yourself and live meaningfully. Ideally, it is best to do this while you are still in bed and, as you place your feet on the floor to get out of bed, consciously stepping into your day with attention, gratitude, and optimism.

2. Before your day gets busy, take a little time for reflection and meditation. During your daily reflection, dedicate a portion of the time to an accurate assessment of your life. The following three thoughts are merely suggestions. If you find all three or any one of them beneficial, include them in your morning reflection/contemplation time.

- Reflect on how fortunate you are to have a life in recovery. While so many in our world are overwhelmed by their addiction, you have found recovery and the freedom from suffering that it offers. You can heal your relationships and be of real benefit to others. Beyond those who suffer from addiction, many people don't even have the opportunity to have an education, clean drinking water in their own homes, or the freedom to make choices in their own lives. Bring to mind people and things you are grateful for. Make them relevant and personal.

- Remember that you are not the center of the universe but a valuable part of it. The events that happen in your life, whether you label them good or bad, are all opportunities to grow, learn, and make your life more meaningful. Life is messy for everyone. It is filled with both joys and sorrows for all of us. No one is immune from hardships and difficulties. In fact, it is only through the challenges you face that you develop your highest qualities.

- You have a life of recovery filled with support and opportunities. Every day is a new opportunity and fresh start if you choose to take advantage of it. Take some time to reflect on the person you want to be. What is a meaningful life to you? How do you want to live this day? Set your intention to not waste this day and live it with attention and intention, cultivating the qualities that you find meaningful. Remember, the only thing that separates the person you are from the person you want to be are the actions you take. Make a clear and firm commitment to your recovery today. You deserve to live a life free of addiction.

3. To cultivate attention in your life, it is important to establish a consistent meditation practice. If you are just starting a practice, do not try to do too much too soon. Quality is much more important than quantity. Start with a shorter period and gradually increase your meditation time.

4. If you pray, include time for your morning prayers. This need not be a religious act; prayer can also include making commitments to your recovery, doing your best to engage in wholesome and meaningful activities, or simply affirming a willingness to be more open and less self-centered.

5. After your meditation, take a little time to read and reflect upon a specific intention for the day. Use this guidebook to engage with the daily lessons and activities. Set an intention you find meaningful and do your best.

6. At the end of the day, take a few minutes to reflect upon the day. Use this guidebook to note what went well and what you would like to improve. If there was something that you did not handle skillfully, take a few moments to reflect upon what happened and how you would like to handle it more skillfully the next time. Set a strong intention to handle it skillfully when it arises again. The "Transforming Unskillful Events" meditation can help you with this. Remember to be gentle with yourself and that this is practice, not perfection.

7. Before bed, again set your intention to wake up and dedicate some time in the morning to your mindfulness practice.

VALUES

"As a single footstep will not make a path on the earth, so a single thought will not make a pathway in the mind. To make a deep physical path, we walk again and again. To make a deep mental path, we must think over and over the kind of thoughts we wish to dominate our lives."

HENRY DAVID THOREAU

Step Two—Returning to Sanity: Living in Alignment with Our Values

The primary symptom of our addictive thinking is a consistent habit of choosing a short-term, stimulus-driven pleasure over lasting happiness. In our confusion and desire to find a way to feel good, we mistakenly believe that we can somehow find a lasting happiness by focusing primarily on activities that give pleasurable feelings. In doing so, we fall into the trap of confusing pleasurable feelings with genuine happiness. This is where the insanity begins. Due to this insanity, we wind up seeking happiness in all the wrong places and doing things that rob us of our dignity, self-worth, and inner joy.

The way we cultivate genuine happiness is not by collecting a long list of pleasurable experiences. It comes from within us and is cultivated by making healthy choices that are based in reality, aligned with our values, and beneficial to ourselves and others. In essence, we cultivate our genuine happiness by living a meaningful life. When we participate in life in a way that we feel good about, in alignment with our values, we find inner peace regardless of the outcome or external circumstances. Conversely, when our actions violate our personal values, we don't feel good about ourselves, regardless of the outcome or circumstances.

We can do things that don't feel pleasurable, which develop integrity and honor within us. We can also do things which are pleasurable but result in feelings of shame and regret. In our insanity, we consistently engage in activities that we hope will make us feel good instead of activities that we will feel good about. Returning to sanity, we remember that we find our worthiness and value by doing things that are worthy and valuable.

Living a life of integrity, in alignment with our values, creates inner peace, well-being, and a meaningful life that supports our recovery. If we are going to flourish in our recovery, we need to explore, investigate, and discover what our deepest values are and what a meaningful life means to us. If we are to be guided by our values, we need to know what they are and bear them in mind as we engage in our lives. As the quote by Thoreau points out, bearing our values in mind does not happen on its own. It takes a conscious effort.

The quotes, lessons, and activities in the Values section will help you identify and clarify your personal values and explore ways you can bring them into your daily activities. This is something we need to bring to our minds repeatedly in all our activities and throughout our days. In doing so, we develop our highest potential by developing the habit of being guided by the principles we hold dearest. If we do not consciously cultivate this habit, we lose track of our deepest values, and our old habits return as we get busy with our daily activities. To develop ourselves and live a purposeful life in recovery requires some personal time of reflection and constant, mindful observation of our activities and experiences.

Values Exercise One

Earlier you identified six values that were most important to you and gave an example of how you felt when you lived up to them. Now return to those same values and give an example of when you engaged in activities that were in direct contradiction to each one.

1. _____

   _____

2. _____

_____

3. _____

_____

4. _____

_____

5. _____

_____

6. _____

_____

How did you feel after going against each value? How does this compare with your previous example of living up to your values?

1. _____

_____

2. _____

_____

3. _____

_____

4. _____

_____

5. _____

_____

6. _____

_____

For each of your previous examples, do your best to explain why you went against your values. Try to look deeply and explain what motivated you and what needs you were trying to meet. Were your needs met?

1. _____

_____

2. _____

_____

3. _____

_____

4. _____

_____

5. _____

_____

6. _____

_____

Returning to your earlier description of the person you want to become, how did your actions undermine the qualities you want to embody in your life?

_____

_____

_____

_____

_____

Values Exercise Two

"… ask me what I think is keeping me from living
fully for the thing I want to live for."

THOMAS MERTON

This quote by the renowned theologian Thomas Merton, invites us to ask ourselves possibly the two most important questions of our lives: What is it that we find truly meaningful and worth living for? And what is preventing us from living fully for the thing we want to live for?

Even though they are of such great importance to our lives, among all the decisions and reflections we make every day, these questions may rarely arise. One consistent answer for nearly all of us regarding the question of what prevents us from living fully for the things we want to live for is simply that we don't know what those things are. We rarely ask ourselves the question or spend much time reflecting deeply on what we want to live for.

If we are to know ourselves and fully live lives in recovery that we find meaningful, it is essential that we spend some time every day reflecting on what that means to us. When considering our lives, defining our values, and learning from our daily actions and interactions, we learn which habits, attitudes, and tendencies either support or diminish the lives we want to live. In essence, this is living mindfully.

The first few activities you completed encouraged you to engage in such a process. However, if you are to make real progress, you need to be consistent, taking time every morning to reflect on who you are and the qualities you want to develop and becoming aware of what prevents you from developing them. Without consistency and bringing these questions to mind repeatedly, they can fall away from your consciousness as you get distracted by the mundane busyness of your life. To live a life you find meaningful, you ultimately must be mindful of whether your values are translated into actions throughout the day.

Purposeful living is a practice, not a philosophy. It is truly an inside job that requires intention and effort. The good news is that it is achievable. It begins with first simply asking the questions. Then take a little time to nourish your reflections and bring some light to the life you want to live. Then, little by little, you do your best to start living them. As obstacles arise, you are now able to recognize them and learn from them. If you are consistent, your answers will come and you will learn the skills to fully develop the life you find worth living.

Reflect upon the quote by Thomas Merton. What are you living for? Answer in detail to the best of your ability.

_____

_____

_____

_____

_____

What is keeping you from living the life you want to live? Identify specific attitudes, habits, and tendencies and explain how they are blocking you.

_____

_____

_____

_____

_____

Identify two values that support the life you want to live and two habits or attitudes that don't. Do your best today to incorporate the supportive ones and avoid the unsupportive ones. For the next week, note specifically when you are able to do this and when you are not.

Value 1. _____

Value 2. _____

Harmful Habits / Attitude 1. _____

Harmful Habits / Attitude 2. _____

Using the Daily Check-Ins

A key component of this guidebook is the daily check-ins. If you are to transform yourself and develop healthy habits that support the person you want to be, you need to identify which habits and tendencies do support you, as well as those that do not. The daily check-ins are invaluable tools as they bring awareness to the skillful actions and attitudes you want to grow and the unskillful ones you want to avoid.

Since you may not want or be able to carry the guidebook with you at all times, you may find it helpful to use a pocket notepad or an app on your smartphone to note your check-ins throughout the day. You can then transfer your observations into the guidebook during your evening reflection time. We have notepads as well as other tips and resources for using the guidebook available on our website at mindfulnessinrecovery.com.

Daily Practice: Values Week One

DAY ONE	DATE:

Morning Prayers and/or Reflection

MORNING REFLECTION

- You have a life of recovery filled with support and opportunities. Every day is a new opportunity and fresh start if you choose to take advantage of it.

- Remember that you are not the center of the universe but a valuable part of it. The events that happen in your life, whether you label them good or bad, are all opportunities to grow, learn, and make your life more meaningful.

- Bring to mind people and things you are grateful for. Make them relevant and personal.

- Take some time to reflect on the person you want to be. Set your intention to not waste this day and live it with attention and intention, cultivating the qualities that you find meaningful. Remember, the only thing that separates the person you are from the person you want to be is the action you take. Make a clear and firm commitment to your recovery today. You deserve to live a life free of addiction.

MORNING MEDITATION

Did you do it? _____ How long? _____

Values _____

Harmful Habits / Attitudes _____

Set a clear intention to focus on the values you want to incorporate into your life and bear in mind the unhealthy attitudes/habits you want to avoid. Do your best to uphold your values and avoid unhealthy attitudes/habits. Remember to be as honest as possible and be easy on yourself. This is a practice to start identifying what you need to work on. The goal is not to be perfect; it is to gather clear information and start making progress toward becoming the person you want to be.

Check in three times a day, noting which actions were skillful and supported your values and which ones were unskillful. Check in once in the morning (before noon), once in the afternoon (before 5:00 p.m.), and once in the evening. These should be short notes, allowing you to remember them for your evening review.

MORNING CHECK-IN

Skillful: _____

Unskillful: _____

AFTERNOON CHECK-IN

Skillful: _____

Unskillful: _____

EVENING CHECK-IN

Skillful: _____

Unskillful: _____

EVENING REVIEW

Reflecting on your day, what did you do well that supported your recovery, values, and the person you want to be?

_____

_____

What did you do that was unskillful, undermining your recovery, values, and the person you want to be?

_____

_____

How can you make amends for, or improve upon, the unskillful actions of today?

_____

_____

DAY TWO   DATE:

Morning Prayers and/or Reflection

MORNING REFLECTION

- You have a life of recovery filled with support and opportunities. Every day is a new opportunity and fresh start if you choose to take advantage of it.

- Remember that you are not the center of the universe but a valuable part of it. The events that happen in your life, whether you label them good or bad, are all opportunities to grow, learn, and make your life more meaningful.

- Bring to mind people and things you are grateful for. Make them relevant and personal.

- Take some time to reflect on the person you want to be. Set your intention to not waste this day and live it with attention and intention, cultivating the qualities that you find meaningful. Remember, the only thing that separates the person you are from the person you want to be is the action you take. Make a clear and firm commitment to your recovery today. You deserve to live a life free of addiction.

MORNING MEDITATION

Did you do it? _____   How long? _____

Values _____

Harmful Habits / Attitudes _____

Set a clear intention to focus on the values you want to incorporate into your life and bear in mind the unhealthy attitudes/habits you want to avoid. Do your best to uphold your values and avoid unhealthy attitudes/habits. Remember to be as honest as possible and be easy on yourself. This is a practice to start identifying what you need to work on. The goal is not to be perfect; it is to gather clear information and start making progress toward becoming the person you want to be.

Check in three times a day, noting what actions were skillful and supported your values and which ones were unskillful. Check in once in the morning (before noon), once in the afternoon (before 5:00 p.m.), and once in the evening. These should be short notes, allowing you to remember them for your evening review.

MORNING CHECK-IN

Skillful: _____

Unskillful: _____

AFTERNOON CHECK-IN

Skillful: _____

Unskillful: _____

EVENING CHECK-IN

Skillful: _____

Unskillful: _____

EVENING REVIEW

Reflecting on your day, what did you do well that supported your recovery, values, and the person you want to be?

_____

_____

What did you do that was unskillful, undermining your recovery, values, and the person you want to be?

_____

_____

How can you make amends for, or improve upon, the unskillful actions of today?

_____

_____

DAY THREE   DATE:

Morning Prayers and/or Reflection

MORNING REFLECTION

- You have a life of recovery filled with support and opportunities. Every day is a new opportunity and fresh start if you choose to take advantage of it.

- Remember that you are not the center of the universe but a valuable part of it. The events that happen in your life, whether you label them good or bad, are all opportunities to grow, learn, and make your life more meaningful.

- Bring to mind people and things you are grateful for. Make them relevant and personal.

- Take some time to reflect on the person you want to be. Set your intention to not waste this day and live it with attention and intention, cultivating the qualities that you find meaningful. Remember, the only thing that separates the person you are from the person you want to be is the action you take. Make a clear and firm commitment to your recovery today. You deserve to live a life free of addiction.

MORNING MEDITATION

Did you do it? _____   How long? _____

Values _____

Harmful Habits / Attitudes _____

Set a clear intention to focus on the values you want to incorporate into your life and bear in mind the unhealthy attitudes/habits you want to avoid. Do your best to uphold your values and avoid unhealthy attitudes/habits. Remember to be as honest as possible and be easy on yourself. This is a practice to start identifying what you need to work on. The goal is not to be perfect; it is to gather clear information and start making progress toward becoming the person you want to be.

Check in three times a day, noting what actions were skillful and supported your values and which ones were unskillful. Check in once in the morning (before noon), once in the afternoon (before 5:00 p.m.), and once in the evening. These should be short notes, allowing you to remember them for your evening review.

MORNING CHECK-IN

Skillful: _____

Unskillful: _____

AFTERNOON CHECK-IN

Skillful: _____

Unskillful: _____

EVENING CHECK-IN

Skillful: _____

Unskillful: _____

EVENING REVIEW

Reflecting on your day, what did you do well that supported your recovery, values, and the person you want to be?

_____

_____

What did you do that was unskillful, undermining your recovery, values, and the person you want to be?

_____

_____

How can you make amends for, or improve upon, the unskillful actions of today?

_____

_____

DAY FOUR   **DATE:**

Morning Prayers and/or Reflection

MORNING REFLECTION

- You have a life of recovery filled with support and opportunities. Every day is a new opportunity and fresh start if you choose to take advantage of it.

- Remember that you are not the center of the universe but a valuable part of it. The events that happen in your life, whether you label them good or bad, are all opportunities to grow, learn, and make your life more meaningful.

- Bring to mind people and things you are grateful for. Make them relevant and personal.

- Take some time to reflect on the person you want to be. Set your intention to not waste this day and live it with attention and intention, cultivating the qualities that you find meaningful. Remember, the only thing that separates the person you are from the person you want to be is the action you take. Make a clear and firm commitment to your recovery today. You deserve to live a life free of addiction.

MORNING MEDITATION

Did you do it? _____   How long? _____

Values _____

Harmful Habits / Attitudes _____

Set a clear intention to focus on the values you want to incorporate into your life and bear in mind the unhealthy attitudes/habits you want to avoid. Do your best to uphold your values and avoid unhealthy attitudes/habits. Remember to be as honest as possible and be easy on yourself. This is a practice to start identifying what you need to work on. The goal is not to be perfect; it is to gather clear information and start making progress toward becoming the person you want to be.

Check in three times a day, noting what actions were skillful and supported your values and which ones were unskillful. Check in once in the morning (before noon), once in the afternoon (before 5:00 p.m.), and once in the evening. These should be short notes, allowing you to remember them for your evening review.

MORNING CHECK-IN

Skillful: _____

Unskillful: _____

AFTERNOON CHECK-IN

Skillful: _____

Unskillful: _____

EVENING CHECK-IN

Skillful: _____

Unskillful: _____

EVENING REVIEW

Reflecting on your day, what did you do well that supported your recovery, values, and the person you want to be?

_____

_____

What did you do that was unskillful, undermining your recovery, values, and the person you want to be?

_____

_____

How can you make amends for, or improve upon, the unskillful actions of today?

_____

_____

DAY FIVE   **DATE:**

Morning Prayers and/or Reflection

MORNING REFLECTION

- You have a life of recovery filled with support and opportunities. Every day is a new opportunity and fresh start if you choose to take advantage of it.

- Remember that you are not the center of the universe but a valuable part of it. The events that happen in your life, whether you label them good or bad, are all opportunities to grow, learn, and make your life more meaningful.

- Bring to mind people and things you are grateful for. Make them relevant and personal.

- Take some time to reflect on the person you want to be. Set your intention to not waste this day and live it with attention and intention, cultivating the qualities that you find meaningful. Remember, the only thing that separates the person you are from the person you want to be is the action you take. Make a clear and firm commitment to your recovery today. You deserve to live a life free of addiction.

MORNING MEDITATION

Did you do it? _____ How long? _____

Values _____

Harmful Habits / Attitudes _____

Set a clear intention to focus on the values you want to incorporate into your life and bear in mind the unhealthy attitudes/habits you want to avoid. Do your best to uphold your values and avoid unhealthy attitudes/habits. Remember to be as honest as possible and be easy on yourself. This is a practice to start identifying what you need to work on. The goal is not to be perfect; it is to gather clear information and start making progress toward becoming the person you want to be.

Check in three times a day, noting what actions were skillful and supported your values and which ones were unskillful. Check in once in the morning (before noon), once in the afternoon (before 5:00 p.m.), and once in the evening. These should be short notes, allowing you to remember them for your evening review.

MORNING CHECK-IN

Skillful: _____

Unskillful: _____

AFTERNOON CHECK-IN

Skillful: _____

Unskillful: _____

EVENING CHECK-IN

Skillful: _____

Unskillful: _____

EVENING REVIEW

Reflecting on your day, what did you do well that supported your recovery, values, and the person you want to be?

_____

_____

What did you do that was unskillful, undermining your recovery, values, and the person you want to be?

_____

_____

How can you make amends for, or improve upon, the unskillful actions of today?

_____

_____

DAY SIX   **DATE:**

Morning Prayers and/or Reflection

MORNING REFLECTION

- You have a life of recovery filled with support and opportunities. Every day is a new opportunity and fresh start if you choose to take advantage of it.

- Remember that you are not the center of the universe but a valuable part of it. The events that happen in your life, whether you label them good or bad, are all opportunities to grow, learn, and make your life more meaningful.

- Bring to mind people and things you are grateful for. Make them relevant and personal.

- Take some time to reflect on the person you want to be. Set your intention to not waste this day and live it with attention and intention, cultivating the qualities that you find meaningful. Remember, the only thing that separates the person you are from the person you want to be is the action you take. Make a clear and firm commitment to your recovery today. You deserve to live a life free of addiction.

MORNING MEDITATION

Did you do it? _____   How long? _____

Values _____

Harmful Habits / Attitudes _____

Set a clear intention to focus on the values you want to incorporate into your life and bear in mind the unhealthy attitudes/habits you want to avoid. Do your best to uphold your values and avoid unhealthy attitudes/habits. Remember to be as honest as possible and be easy on yourself. This is a practice to start identifying what you need to work on. The goal is not to be perfect; it is to gather clear information and start making progress toward becoming the person you want to be.

Check in three times a day, noting what actions were skillful and supported your values and which ones were unskillful. Check in once in the morning (before noon), once in the afternoon (before 5:00 p.m.), and once in the evening. These should be short notes, allowing you to remember them for your evening review.

MORNING CHECK-IN

Skillful: _____

Unskillful: _____

AFTERNOON CHECK-IN

Skillful: _____

Unskillful: _____

EVENING CHECK-IN

Skillful: _____

Unskillful: _____

EVENING REVIEW

Reflecting on your day, what did you do well that supported your recovery, values, and the person you want to be?

_____

_____

What did you do that was unskillful, undermining your recovery, values, and the person you want to be?

_____

_____

How can you make amends for, or improve upon, the unskillful actions of today?

_____

_____

DAY SEVEN   **DATE:**

Morning Prayers and/or Reflection

MORNING REFLECTION

- You have a life of recovery filled with support and opportunities. Every day is a new opportunity and fresh start if you choose to take advantage of it.

- Remember that you are not the center of the universe but a valuable part of it. The events that happen in your life, whether you label them good or bad, are all opportunities to grow, learn, and make your life more meaningful.

- Bring to mind people and things you are grateful for. Make them relevant and personal.

- Take some time to reflect on the person you want to be. Set your intention to not waste this day and live it with attention and intention, cultivating the qualities that you find meaningful. Remember, the only thing that separates the person you are from the person you want to be is the action you take. Make a clear and firm commitment to your recovery today. You deserve to live a life free of addiction.

MORNING MEDITATION

Did you do it? _____   How long? _____

Values _____

Harmful Habits / Attitudes _____

Set a clear intention to focus on the values you want to incorporate into your life and bear in mind the unhealthy attitudes/habits you want to avoid. Do your best to uphold your values and avoid unhealthy attitudes/habits. Remember to be as honest as possible and be easy on yourself. This is a practice to start identifying what you need to work on. The goal is not to be perfect; it is to gather clear information and start making progress toward becoming the person you want to be.

Check in three times a day, noting what actions were skillful and supported your values and which ones were unskillful. Check in once in the morning (before noon), once in the afternoon (before 5:00 p.m.), and once in the evening. These should be short notes, allowing you to remember them for your evening review.

MORNING CHECK-IN

Skillful: _____

Unskillful: _____

AFTERNOON CHECK-IN

Skillful: _____

Unskillful: _____

EVENING CHECK-IN

Skillful: _____

Unskillful: _____

EVENING REVIEW

Reflecting on your day, what did you do well that supported your recovery, values, and the person you want to be?

_____

_____

What did you do that was unskillful, undermining your recovery, values, and the person you want to be?

_____

_____

How can you make amends for, or improve upon, the unskillful actions of today?

_____

_____

VALUES REVIEW

Looking back over the last week, what did you discover about yourself?

_____

_____

_____

What were some of the good qualities you noticed in yourself that you would like to grow?

_____

_____

_____

What were some of the attitudes or habits that you found difficult to avoid?

_____

_____

_____

What did you do well this week that supports your recovery?

_____

_____

_____

What would you like to improve?

_____

_____

_____

ATTENTION

Step One Explored: We do not need to be powerless over every thought, feeling, or impulse we have.

We can develop more choice and the ability to respond consciously rather than react habitually to every thought, feeling, impulse, or desire that arises. We do not need to remain powerless, or unable to make healthy choices, when our disease speaks to us.

By far, one of the biggest obstacles to finding recovery and developing our highest potential is our untrained mind. Unless we consciously train our mind, developing the ability to direct our attention where we choose to, it will endlessly drag us from one thought to another.

The mind continuously produces thoughts and images. Try to not think for one minute and see what happens. It's one thing to constantly have mental activity, but the bigger problem is that the mind compulsively draws our attention away from what we are doing and toward the thoughts and images it produces. It draws us in, tells us what to worry about, stress over, desire, and ruminate upon. It constantly distracts us from our current activity and intention. A study by psychologists Matthew A. Killingsworth and Daniel T. Gilbert of Harvard University showed that most people are so distracted that they do not know what they are doing about half the time they are awake.

Therefore, we don't know where our car keys are sometimes. Our mind was somewhere else when we put them down. If we are going to establish free will and make healthy choices that support our recovery, we need to be present in the moments of our lives.

So much of our lives go by without us being present. How much of our days are we able to actually be in the present moment? At its core, mindfulness is the ability to be fully present in the moments of our lives, attending to them with wisdom and clarity, being able to initiate actions and respond to whatever arises in ways that support our recovery and are healthy and meaningful to us. The first step is learning to pay attention in our own lives.

Attention Exercise One

"Remember, everyone you meet is really trying to do the best they can. No one woke up today and intentionally decided to be mean, difficult, or unreasonable—including you."

JOHN BRUNA

One of the most important things we can pay attention to in our recovery is our attitude and judgments regarding ourselves and others. If we are not mindful, we can easily become the center of our own universe, making our personal desires a priority over all others. In the process, we start judging and labeling others as good or bad in relation to whether they are helping us meet our needs and desires or whether they are blocking us from our goals. What emerges are three categories of people: the ones we like because they meet our needs in some way, the ones we do not like because they don't meet our needs, and the ones we are neutral about because they have not affected us much either way. Essentially, we like the people who help us, who share our values, or who we find fun to be around, which can be a limiting and divisive habit. Our friends can instantly become enemies and those we dislike can become friends, based simply on whether they benefit us or not.

When we are the most important person in the world, we are instantly in conflict with everyone else, who, just like us, is trying to get their needs met and lead happy lives. If we can remember that all others are trying to find their way just like us, we can also remember that they have struggles, worries, and concerns just like us. In truth, we are all in this together, and our well-being depends upon one another. Everything we have—from our food, clothing, education, home, and so on—is because of others. People we have never met, who have suffered in ways we cannot imagine, have provided the labor and conditions for us to enjoy the lives we have today, building our schools, growing our food, and making our clothes.

It is helpful to watch our minds, bringing our attention to how we judge ourselves and others. Remember that no one label, or judgment, could ever tell the whole story of any person. Each day we all wake up and try to find a way to get our needs met. We all make mistakes, let people down, help people, and improve our own lives. It is much healthier and more accurate to remember that the labels we apply to ourselves and others capture only a moment. When people are having a bad moment, it is a reflection of their current struggle and not who they really are. If we look deeply, it is difficult to find someone who has not helped us in some way.

Today be mindful of your judgments of others. Try to separate the things people do from the people they are. Of course, people are accountable for what they do, but those few actions can never define them. Do your best to remember that, in general, all people are really doing the best they can, and all of them have endured hardships you will never know. Try to be a good team member in this thing we call life.

ATTENTION EXERCISE ONE   DATE:

Morning Prayers and/or Reflection

MORNING REFLECTION

- You have a life of recovery filled with support and opportunities. Every day is a new opportunity and fresh start if you choose to take advantage of it.

- Remember that you are not the center of the universe but a valuable part of it. The events that happen in your life, whether you label them good or bad, are all opportunities to grow, learn, and make your life more meaningful.

- Bring to mind people and things you are grateful for. Make them relevant and personal.

- Take some time to reflect on the person you want to be. Set your intention to not waste this day and live it with attention and intention, cultivating the qualities that you find meaningful. Remember, the only thing that separates the person you are from the person you want to be is the action you take. Make a clear and firm commitment to your recovery today. You deserve to live a life free of addiction.

MORNING MEDITATION

Did you do it? _____ How long? _____

Set a clear intention to focus on the judgments you make about yourself and others. How do your judgments affect your mood and interactions? If you change your judgment, does that change your interactions?

Check in three times a day, noting what actions were skillful and unskillful regarding your judgments. Check in once in the morning (before noon), once in the afternoon (before 5:00 p.m.), and once in the evening. These should be short notes, allowing you to remember them for your evening review.

MORNING CHECK-IN

Skillful: _____

Unskillful: _____

AFTERNOON CHECK-IN

Skillful: _____

Unskillful: _____

EVENING CHECK-IN

Skillful: _____

Unskillful: _____

EVENING REVIEW

Reflecting on your day, what did you learn about your judgments that were positive?

_____

_____

When you noticed a judgment, what did you do that was unskillful that you would like to change?

_____

_____

How can you make amends for, or improve upon, the unskillful actions of today?

_____

_____

Attention Exercise Two

"You have power over your mind—not outside events.
Realize this, and you will find strength."

MARCUS AURELIUS

With all the ups and downs of our daily lives, it is easy to forget that the events themselves are not the cause of our happiness or suffering. The real cause is how we perceive and relate to these events. This does not mean the ups and downs do not have an effect. Clearly, they do; however, the degree and manner in which they affect us is primarily a result of our attitude toward them.

Difficulties can be perceived as challenges or as opportunities. Likewise, opportunities can seem like too much work for us to bother with, or they can offer us great hope. It all depends on our attitude and what we choose to pay attention to.

Our experiences are also affected by how we are feeling when they happen. When we feel great, very little seems to bother us. When we feel terrible, even things we normally enjoy can bring us no pleasure. How we see the world we live in is always subjective. While we do not have control over of the world, we do have control over how we experience it.

What we attend to becomes important to us. If we are constantly attending to how happy we would be "if only this or that would happen," we create dissatisfaction in the current moment. If we attend to the reality of our current moment, we may find that it offers us all that we really need, and we already have a long list of things to be grateful for. We may also remember that each moment is precious, for it will never come again.

We can learn to bring our attention back to the one thing we have some direct power over: our attitude. Every event and interaction in our lives, whether painful or pleasurable, offers us the opportunity to improve ourselves and the world we live in. Imagine cultivating that truth as an ongoing attitude.

Today work on adjusting your attitude throughout the day. See if you can adopt an attitude of gratitude and maintain it all day. Everyone you meet and everything that happens to you today is an opportunity for you to improve yourself and develop the tools of recovery. If people and events create challenges, see if you can rise to meet them, developing your inner strength and character. If they are pleasant, enjoy them and share your joy with others. Do not stuff feelings or ignore problems but acknowledge them and learn from them.

ATTENTION EXERCISE TWO   **DATE:**

Morning Prayers and/or Reflection

MORNING REFLECTION

- You have a life of recovery filled with support and opportunities. Every day is a new opportunity and fresh start if you choose to take advantage of it.

- Remember that you are not the center of the universe but a valuable part of it. The events that happen in your life, whether you label them good or bad, are all opportunities to grow, learn, and make your life more meaningful.

- Bring to mind people and things you are grateful for. Make them relevant and personal.

- Take some time to reflect on the person you want to be. Set your intention to not waste this day and live it with attention and intention, cultivating the qualities that you find meaningful. Remember, the only thing that separates the person you are from the person you want to be is the action you take. Make a clear and firm commitment to your recovery today. You deserve to live a life free of addiction.

MORNING MEDITATION

Did you do it? _____   How long? _____

Just for today, set a clear intention to do your best to cultivate and maintain an attitude of gratitude. Notice how that affects your interactions and activities. What happens when your attitude changes?

Check in three times a day, noting what actions were skillful and unskillful regarding your attitude. Check in once in the morning (before noon), once in the afternoon (before 5:00 p.m.), and once in the evening. These should be short notes, allowing you to remember them for your evening review.

MORNING CHECK-IN

Skillful: _____

Unskillful: _____

AFTERNOON CHECK-IN

Skillful: _____

Unskillful: _____

EVENING CHECK-IN

Skillful: _____

Unskillful: _____

EVENING REVIEW

Reflecting on your day, what did you learn about yourself?

_____

_____

Was it difficult to maintain an attitude of gratitude? Why or why not?

_____

_____

How can you make amends for, or improve upon, the unskillful actions of today?

_____

_____

Attention Exercise Three

"Be wise. Treat yourself, your mind, sympathetically,
with loving kindness. If you are gentle with yourself,
you will become gentle with others."

LAMA YESHE

In our recovery, we are often much harder on ourselves than we are on others. If we pay close attention, we will notice an inner dialogue that evaluates our abilities, activities, and interactions. While this is necessary to some degree—we need to have an awareness of our strengths, weaknesses, and areas of growth—it can become overly critical and unrealistic.

Instead of being a supportive friend, reminding us of our growth and encouraging us to keep developing our potential, our inner voice can become a critic, constantly comparing us with others and reminding us of our shortcomings. This leads to a case of the "shoulds": "I should be more like that"; "I should have done it that way"; "I should have known better"; "I never should have tried that." This constant inner critic only creates separation and more dissatisfaction.

If we can bring attention to our inner dialogue, we can direct it in a more realistic and supportive way. We can remind ourselves that our goal is not to be better than other people but to be better than our previous selves. Our supportive inner voice does not need to dwell on a mistake. Instead, it can remind us that mistakes are opportunities to learn. Everyone makes mistakes, and, in truth, our mistakes are incredibly few compared with all the things we do successfully every day. There really is no contest. When we are gentle with ourselves, we remember that, just like everyone else, we are doing our best and learning along the way. Instead of constantly comparing ourselves with others, we get to learn from and with them. The more we are truly accepting of ourselves the less we need to prove ourselves to others. This creates healthier and more authentic interactions.

For the next three days, pay attention to your inner dialogue. Make sure it is a supportive and realistic conversation. Notice when it is not and see if you can change the conversation.

ATTENTION EXERCISE THREE, DAY ONE   **DATE:**

Morning Prayers and/or Reflection

MORNING REFLECTION

- You have a life of recovery filled with support and opportunities. Every day is a new opportunity and fresh start if you choose to take advantage of it.

- Remember that you are not the center of the universe but a valuable part of it. The events that happen in your life, whether you label them good or bad, are all opportunities to grow, learn, and make your life more meaningful.

- Bring to mind people and things you are grateful for. Make them relevant and personal.

- Take some time to reflect on the person you want to be. Set your intention to not waste this day and live it with attention and intention, cultivating the qualities that you find meaningful. Remember, the only thing that separates the person you are from the person you want to be is the action you take. Make a clear and firm commitment to your recovery today. You deserve to live a life free of addiction.

MORNING MEDITATION

Did you do it? _____   How long? _____

Set a clear intention and do your best to pay attention to your inner dialogue. Make sure it is a supportive and realistic conversation. When you notice it is not, see if you can change the conversation.

Check in three times a day, noting what actions were skillful and unskillful regarding your inner dialogue. Check in once in the morning (before noon), once in the afternoon (before 5:00 p.m.), and once in the evening. These should be short notes, allowing you to remember them for your evening review.

MORNING CHECK-IN

Skillful: _____

Unskillful: _____

AFTERNOON CHECK-IN

Skillful: _____

Unskillful: _____

EVENING CHECK-IN

Skillful: _____

Unskillful: _____

EVENING REVIEW

Reflecting on your day, what did you learn about yourself?

_____

_____

Describe some of the healthy thoughts and conversations that you found helpful.

_____

_____

Describe some of the unhealthy thoughts and conversations that arose. Were you able to change the conversation?

_____

_____

How can you make amends for, or improve upon, the unskillful actions of today?

_____

_____

ATTENTION EXERCISE THREE, DAY TWO   DATE:

Morning Prayers and/or Reflection

MORNING REFLECTION

- You have a life of recovery filled with support and opportunities. Every day is a new opportunity and fresh start if you choose to take advantage of it.

- Remember that you are not the center of the universe but a valuable part of it. The events that happen in your life, whether you label them good or bad, are all opportunities to grow, learn, and make your life more meaningful.

- Bring to mind people and things you are grateful for. Make them relevant and personal.

- Take some time to reflect on the person you want to be. Set your intention to not waste this day and live it with attention and intention, cultivating the qualities that you find meaningful. Remember, the only thing that separates the person you are from the person you want to be is the action you take. Make a clear and firm commitment to your recovery today. You deserve to live a life free of addiction.

MORNING MEDITATION

Did you do it? _____   How long? _____

Set a clear intention and do your best to pay attention to your inner dialogue. Make sure it is a supportive and realistic conversation. When you notice when it is not, see if you can change the conversation.

Check in three times a day, noting what actions were skillful and unskillful regarding your inner dialogue. Check in once in the morning (before noon), once in the afternoon (before 5:00 p.m.), and once in the evening. These should be short notes, allowing you to remember them for your evening review.

MORNING CHECK-IN

Skillful: _____

Unskillful: _____

AFTERNOON CHECK-IN

Skillful: _____

Unskillful: _____

EVENING CHECK-IN

Skillful: _____

Unskillful: _____

EVENING REVIEW

Reflecting on your day, what did you learn about yourself?

_____

_____

Describe some of the healthy thoughts and conversations that you found helpful.

_____

_____

Describe some of the unhealthy thoughts and conversations that arose. Were you able to change the conversation?

_____

_____

How can you make amends for, or improve upon, the unskillful actions of today?

_____

_____

ATTENTION EXERCISE THREE, DAY THREE   **DATE:**

Morning Prayers and/or Reflection

MORNING REFLECTION

- You have a life of recovery filled with support and opportunities. Every day is a new opportunity and fresh start if you choose to take advantage of it.

- Remember that you are not the center of the universe but a valuable part of it. The events that happen in your life, whether you label them good or bad, are all opportunities to grow, learn, and make your life more meaningful.

- Bring to mind people and things you are grateful for. Make them relevant and personal.

- Take some time to reflect on the person you want to be. Set your intention to not waste this day and live it with attention and intention, cultivating the qualities that you find meaningful. Remember, the only thing that separates the person you are from the person you want to be is the action you take. Make a clear and firm commitment to your recovery today. You deserve to live a life free of addiction.

MORNING MEDITATION

Did you do it? _____ How long? _____

Set a clear intention and do your best to pay attention to your inner dialogue. Make sure it is a supportive and realistic conversation. When you notice when it is not, see if you can change the conversation.

Check in three times a day, noting what actions were skillful and unskillful regarding your inner dialogue. Check in once in the morning (before noon), once in the afternoon (before 5:00 p.m.), and once in the evening. These should be short notes, allowing you to remember them for your evening review.

MORNING CHECK-IN

Skillful: _____

Unskillful: _____

AFTERNOON CHECK-IN

Skillful: _____

Unskillful: _____

EVENING CHECK-IN

Skillful: _____

Unskillful: _____

EVENING REVIEW

Reflecting on your day, what did you learn about yourself?

_____

_____

Describe some of the healthy thoughts and conversations that you found helpful.

_____

_____

Describe some of the unhealthy thoughts and conversations that arose. Were you able to change the conversation?

_____

_____

How can you make amends for, or improve upon, the unskillful actions of today?

_____

_____

Attention Exercise Four

*"There is wisdom in turning as often as possible
from the familiar to the unfamiliar."*

GEORGE SANTAYANA

It is easy to become complacent, staying in our comfort zone with people, ideas, habits, and activities that are familiar to us. This can create a cocoon that feels safe and stable. It can also dampen our awareness and impede opportunities to grow in our recovery. As you have no doubt learned by now, familiar habits and attitudes are not necessarily healthy or beneficial.

When it comes to people, places, ideas, and things we have labeled "familiar," we often do not pay close attention and easily assume we know all the details, backgrounds, and intricacies associated with them. In fact, we may not be accurate at all. When we contemplate how little attention we actually give them, it begs the question: Is the familiar something we really know all that well?

With the unfamiliar, we will often make guesses or assumptions and believe we know more than we actually do. It is natural that we do this with the unfamiliar, considering that, in our quest for stability, we are constantly trying to identify and label how things are, how they work, and how different types of people or cultures function.

However, our generalizations, assumptions, and even projections about the familiar or unfamiliar—besides being untrue much of the time—prevent us from having an inquisitive nature and sharpening our awareness. The biggest impediment to learning is the presumption of knowledge. When we think we know something or someone, we are no longer inquiring. We can easily forget that, among all the other humans out there, many may have another perspective, understanding, or technique we have never encountered.

Our world is a fascinating place, and every day in recovery there is much to learn, explore, and engage with in meaningful ways—if we are willing and paying attention. In addition, things are constantly changing, and it is healthy, if not essential, to continue increasing our awareness, perspective, and understanding of the world. To grow and flourish, it is important to keep learning.

For the next two days, have an open and inquisitive mind. Try your best to learn something new about the familiar and make an effort to investigate the unfamiliar. Bring an inquisitive mind into your regular activities and interactions.

ATTENTION EXERCISE FOUR, DAY ONE   DATE:

Morning Prayers and/or Reflection

MORNING REFLECTION

- You have a life of recovery filled with support and opportunities. Every day is a new opportunity and fresh start if you choose to take advantage of it.

- Remember that you are not the center of the universe but a valuable part of it. The events that happen in your life, whether you label them good or bad, are all opportunities to grow, learn, and make your life more meaningful.

- Bring to mind people and things you are grateful for. Make them relevant and personal.

- Take some time to reflect on the person you want to be. Set your intention to not waste this day and live it with attention and intention, cultivating the qualities that you find meaningful. Remember, the only thing that separates the person you are from the person you want to be is the action you take. Make a clear and firm commitment to your recovery today. You deserve to live a life free of addiction.

MORNING MEDITATION

Did you do it? _____ How long? _____

Set a clear intention and do your best to have an open and inquisitive mind. Try your best to learn something new about the familiar and make an effort to investigate the unfamiliar. Be open to learning and bring an inquisitive mind into your regular activities and interactions.

Check in three times a day, noting what actions were skillful and unskillful regarding your openness to learning. Check in once in the morning (before noon), once in the afternoon (before 5:00 p.m.), and once in the evening. These should be short notes, allowing you to remember them for your evening review.

MORNING CHECK-IN

Skillful: _____

Unskillful: _____

AFTERNOON CHECK-IN

Skillful: _____

Unskillful: _____

EVENING CHECK-IN

Skillful: _____

Unskillful: _____

EVENING REVIEW

Reflecting on your day, what did you learn?

_____

_____

Was it difficult to have an open mind today? Explain why or why not.

_____

_____

How can you make amends for, or improve upon, the unskillful actions of today?

_____

_____

ATTENTION EXERCISE FOUR, DAY TWO   **DATE:**

Morning Prayers and/or Reflection

MORNING REFLECTION

- You have a life of recovery filled with support and opportunities. Every day is a new opportunity and fresh start if you choose to take advantage of it.

- Remember that you are not the center of the universe but a valuable part of it. The events that happen in your life, whether you label them good or bad, are all opportunities to grow, learn, and make your life more meaningful.

- Bring to mind people and things you are grateful for. Make them relevant and personal.

- Take some time to reflect on the person you want to be. Set your intention to not waste this day and live it with attention and intention, cultivating the qualities that you find meaningful. Remember, the only thing that separates the person you are from the person you want to be is the action you take. Make a clear and firm commitment to your recovery today. You deserve to live a life free of addiction.

MORNING MEDITATION

Did you do it? _____   How long? _____

Set a clear intention and do your best to have an open and inquisitive mind. Try your best to learn something new about the familiar and make an effort to investigate the unfamiliar. Be open to learning and bring an inquisitive mind into your regular activities and interactions.

Check in three times a day, noting what actions were skillful and unskillful regarding your openness to learning. Check in once in the morning (before noon), once in the afternoon (before 5:00 p.m.), and once in the evening. These should be short notes, allowing you to remember them for your evening review.

MORNING CHECK-IN

Skillful: _____

Unskillful: _____

AFTERNOON CHECK-IN

Skillful: _____

Unskillful: _____

EVENING CHECK-IN

Skillful: _____

Unskillful: _____

EVENING REVIEW

Reflecting on your day, what did you learn?

_____

_____

Was it difficult to have an open mind today? Explain why or why not.

_____

_____

How can you make amends for, or improve upon, the unskillful actions of today?

_____

_____

ATTENTION REVIEW

What were the most valuable lessons you learned this week?

_____

_____

_____

What were some of the ways you were able to benefit from choosing to direct your attention?

_____

_____

_____

What did you do well this week that supports your recovery?

_____

_____

_____

What would you like to improve?

_____

_____

_____

WISDOM

Step Three: Recognizing powers greater than ourselves and the suffering we bring upon ourselves through self-centered actions.

"When we quit thinking primarily about ourselves and our own self-preservation, we undergo a truly heroic transformation of consciousness."

JOSEPH CAMPBELL

Essentially, the main cause of our unhappiness is a fundamental misperception of ourselves and the world around us. Despite all evidence to the contrary, our minds present us with a vision of the world that ultimately has little basis in reality. If we want to truly live a meaningful life and cultivate inner peace and genuine happiness, we need to understand the true sources of peace and happiness and develop their conditions in the real world.

A common belief is that we live in a world in which, if we exercise and eat right, we will be healthy and live long; if we maintain our cars, they will not break down; if we cultivate healthy relationships, they will last; and if we work hard and get the right job, we will have security.

However, life is messy in the real world. No matter how healthy our food is or how much we exercise, we can become ill, contract a fatal disease, or die in an accident. Cars can break down even if they are well maintained. Relationships come and go and change over time as well as jobs. These truths apply to everyone.

Our misperception of the world becomes a significant problem because it leaves us ill-prepared to face the realities of life when they occur. Even though we see cancer centers, auto repair shops, marriage and family counselors, and unemployment offices, we somehow think they should not be part of our lives. As a result, we often feel as if we are victims or believe that life is unfair when normal things happen. However, if we understand that these things are part of the nature of life, we are much better able to respond to the challenges and opportunities that present themselves.

This is an extremely critical point. We need to understand clearly the nature of the world we live in if we want to navigate it skillfully. The world we live in has hospitals because people get injured and have illnesses. The world has therapists and counselors because people struggle to get along with each other and interact in the world. There are auto repair shops because cars break down, plumbers because toilets back up, cemeteries because people die, and emergency workers because natural disasters happen. The world we live in has crime, poverty, injustice, and economic fluctuations. This is simply the nature of things.

Despite knowing this, all too often our minds tell us that we won't need a therapist, become ill or injured, have a car break down, be a victim of crime, or die at a young age. It's as if the rules of life don't apply to us. We see these things happen to other people often, yet we firmly believe that they should not happen to us or our loved ones. Consequently, when something does happen, we can feel that life is unfair and ask, "Why me?"

But, why not us? Why should we be exempt from the rules that apply to everyone else? This is the ground from which suffering grows—the belief that things should be different from the way they are or, more precisely, be the way we want them to be.

Wisdom Exercise One

"We cannot change anything until we accept it.
Condemnation does not liberate, it oppresses."

CARL JUNG

Acceptance, instead of being passive, is a liberating and empowering activity. In accepting our addiction and unhealthy behaviors, we found our recovery. With acceptance, we give ourselves permission to live in reality instead of in a state of dissatisfaction, clinging to an idea that things should be different.

As Carl Jung's quote points out, our resistance to accepting things oppresses our ability to improve them. Until we can accept things, we cannot learn from or improve them. Acceptance does not mean that we like what is happening; it means that we have come to terms with reality and are ready to learn from, improve, or make the best of the situation.

When we resist things that have already happened, thinking they should not have happened, we fall into a delusional state that creates unnecessary suffering and prevents us from making healthy choices. Things happen for reasons. Life is messy for everyone. No one is unique in that way.

Ultimately, there are always causes for things that happen, whether we like them or not. So, when we think something should not have happened, we are clearly forgetting that there were causes. The fact that we don't like what happened or do not think that the causes should have happened does not negate the reality that both the causes and results did happen. Once they have happened, no amount of resistance, denial, or condemnation can change that.

The more quickly we are able to accept reality and move into acceptance the more quickly we can move into solution mode and liberate ourselves from the mental anguish caused by delusionally dwelling on how things could have been different. With acceptance, we are empowered to immediately improve our situation, simply by changing our understanding and perspective of it.

For the next week, cultivate wise acceptance. Take an optimistic, problem-solving attitude. When you notice resistance or if things do not go your way, instead of dwelling on how something should have been different, see if you can move into acceptance and improve the situation. See how effectively you can learn to live in the real world, accepting life on life's terms, and welcome what lessons this has to offer you.

WISDOM EXERCISE ONE, DAY ONE   **DATE:**

Morning Prayers and/or Reflection

MORNING REFLECTION

- You have a life of recovery filled with support and opportunities. Every day is a new opportunity and fresh start if you choose to take advantage of it.

- Remember that you are not the center of the universe but a valuable part of it. The events that happen in your life, whether you label them good or bad, are all opportunities to grow, learn, and make your life more meaningful.

- Bring to mind people and things you are grateful for. Make them relevant and personal.

- Take some time to reflect on the person you want to be. Set your intention to not waste this day and live it with attention and intention, cultivating the qualities that you find meaningful. Remember, the only thing that separates the person you are from the person you want to be is the action you take. Make a clear and firm commitment to your recovery today. You deserve to live a life free of addiction.

MORNING MEDITATION

Did you do it? _____   How long? _____

Set a clear intention and do your best to cultivate wise acceptance. Take an optimistic, problem-solving attitude. When you notice resistance or if things do not go your way, instead of dwelling on how something should have been different, see if you can move into acceptance and improve the situation. See how effectively you can learn to live in the real world, accepting life on life's terms, and see what lessons this has to offer you.

Check in three times a day, noting what actions were skillful and unskillful regarding acceptance. Check in once in the morning (before noon), once in the afternoon (before 5:00 p.m.), and once in the evening. These should be short notes, allowing you to remember them for your evening review.

MORNING CHECK-IN

Skillful: _____

Unskillful: _____

AFTERNOON CHECK-IN

Skillful: _____

Unskillful: _____

EVENING CHECK-IN

Skillful: _____

Unskillful: _____

EVENING REVIEW

Reflecting on your day, what did you learn?

_____

_____

What was helpful about acceptance today?

_____

_____

What was difficult about acceptance today?

_____

_____

What did you do well today?

_____

_____

How can you make amends for, or improve upon, the unskillful actions of today?

_____

_____

WISDOM EXERCISE ONE, DAY TWO   DATE:

Morning Prayers and/or Reflection

MORNING REFLECTION

- You have a life of recovery filled with support and opportunities. Every day is a new opportunity and fresh start if you choose to take advantage of it.

- Remember that you are not the center of the universe but a valuable part of it. The events that happen in your life, whether you label them good or bad, are all opportunities to grow, learn, and make your life more meaningful.

- Bring to mind people and things you are grateful for. Make them relevant and personal.

- Take some time to reflect on the person you want to be. Set your intention to not waste this day and live it with attention and intention, cultivating the qualities that you find meaningful. Remember, the only thing that separates the person you are from the person you want to be is the action you take. Make a clear and firm commitment to your recovery today. You deserve to live a life free of addiction.

MORNING MEDITATION

Did you do it? _____   How long? _____

Set a clear intention and do your best to cultivate wise acceptance. Take an optimistic, problem-solving attitude. When you notice resistance or if things do not go your way, instead of dwelling on how something should have been different, see if you can move into acceptance and improve the situation. See how effectively you can learn to live in the real world, accepting life on life's terms, and see what lessons this has to offer you.

Check in three times a day, noting what actions were skillful and unskillful regarding acceptance. Check in once in the morning (before noon), once in the afternoon (before 5:00 p.m.), and once in the evening. These should be short notes, allowing you to remember them for your evening review.

MORNING CHECK-IN

Skillful: _____

Unskillful: _____

AFTERNOON CHECK-IN

Skillful: _____

Unskillful: _____

EVENING CHECK-IN

Skillful: _____

Unskillful: _____

EVENING REVIEW

Reflecting on your day, what did you learn?

_____

_____

What was helpful about acceptance today?

_____

_____

What was difficult about acceptance today?

_____

_____

What did you do well today?

_____

_____

How can you make amends for, or improve upon, the unskillful actions of today?

_____

_____

WISDOM EXERCISE ONE, DAY THREE　　　　　DATE:

Morning Prayers and/or Reflection

MORNING REFLECTION

- You have a life of recovery filled with support and opportunities. Every day is a new opportunity and fresh start if you choose to take advantage of it.

- Remember that you are not the center of the universe but a valuable part of it. The events that happen in your life, whether you label them good or bad, are all opportunities to grow, learn, and make your life more meaningful.

- Bring to mind people and things you are grateful for. Make them relevant and personal.

- Take some time to reflect on the person you want to be. Set your intention to not waste this day and live it with attention and intention, cultivating the qualities that you find meaningful. Remember, the only thing that separates the person you are from the person you want to be is the action you take. Make a clear and firm commitment to your recovery today. You deserve to live a life free of addiction.

MORNING MEDITATION

Did you do it? _____　　How long? _____

Set a clear intention and do your best to cultivate wise acceptance. Take an optimistic, problem-solving attitude. When you notice resistance or if things do not go your way, instead of dwelling on how something should have been different, see if you can move into acceptance and improve the situation. See how effectively you can learn to live in the real world, accepting life on life's terms, and see what lessons this has to offer you.

Check in three times a day, noting what actions were skillful and unskillful regarding acceptance. Check in once in the morning (before noon), once in the afternoon (before 5:00 p.m.), and once in the evening. These should be short notes, allowing you to remember them for your evening review.

MORNING CHECK-IN

Skillful: _____

Unskillful: _____

AFTERNOON CHECK-IN

Skillful: _____

Unskillful: _____

EVENING CHECK-IN

Skillful: _____

Unskillful: _____

EVENING REVIEW

Reflecting on your day, what did you learn?

_____

_____

What was helpful about acceptance today?

_____

_____

What was difficult about acceptance today?

_____

_____

What did you do well today?

_____

_____

How can you make amends for, or improve upon, the unskillful actions of today?

_____

_____

WISDOM EXERCISE ONE, DAY FOUR   **DATE:**

Morning Prayers and/or Reflection

MORNING REFLECTION

- You have a life of recovery filled with support and opportunities. Every day is a new opportunity and fresh start if you choose to take advantage of it.

- Remember that you are not the center of the universe but a valuable part of it. The events that happen in your life, whether you label them good or bad, are all opportunities to grow, learn, and make your life more meaningful.

- Bring to mind people and things you are grateful for. Make them relevant and personal.

- Take some time to reflect on the person you want to be. Set your intention to not waste this day and live it with attention and intention, cultivating the qualities that you find meaningful. Remember, the only thing that separates the person you are from the person you want to be is the action you take. Make a clear and firm commitment to your recovery today. You deserve to live a life free of addiction.

MORNING MEDITATION

Did you do it? _____   How long? _____

Set a clear intention and do your best to cultivate wise acceptance. Take an optimistic, problem-solving attitude. When you notice resistance or if things do not go your way, instead of dwelling on how something should have been different, see if you can move into acceptance and improve the situation. See how effectively you can learn to live in the real world, accepting life on life's terms, and see what lessons this has to offer you.

Check in three times a day, noting what actions were skillful and unskillful regarding acceptance. Check in once in the morning (before noon), once in the afternoon (before 5:00 p.m.), and once in the evening. These should be short notes, allowing you to remember them for your evening review.

MORNING CHECK-IN

Skillful: _____

Unskillful: _____

AFTERNOON CHECK-IN

Skillful: _____

Unskillful: _____

EVENING CHECK-IN

Skillful: _____

Unskillful: _____

EVENING REVIEW

Reflecting on your day, what did you learn?

_____

_____

What was helpful about acceptance today?

_____

_____

What was difficult about acceptance today?

_____

_____

What did you do well today?

_____

_____

How can you make amends for, or improve upon, the unskillful actions of today?

_____

_____

WISDOM EXERCISE ONE, DAY FIVE   DATE:

Morning Prayers and/or Reflection

MORNING REFLECTION

- You have a life of recovery filled with support and opportunities. Every day is a new opportunity and fresh start if you choose to take advantage of it.

- Remember that you are not the center of the universe but a valuable part of it. The events that happen in your life, whether you label them good or bad, are all opportunities to grow, learn, and make your life more meaningful.

- Bring to mind people and things you are grateful for. Make them relevant and personal.

- Take some time to reflect on the person you want to be. Set your intention to not waste this day and live it with attention and intention, cultivating the qualities that you find meaningful. Remember, the only thing that separates the person you are from the person you want to be is the action you take. Make a clear and firm commitment to your recovery today. You deserve to live a life free of addiction.

MORNING MEDITATION

Did you do it? _____   How long? _____

Set a clear intention and do your best to cultivate wise acceptance. Take an optimistic, problem-solving attitude. When you notice resistance or if things do not go your way, instead of dwelling on how something should have been different, see if you can move into acceptance and improve the situation. See how effectively you can learn to live in the real world, accepting life on life's terms, and see what lessons this has to offer you.

Check in three times a day, noting what actions were skillful and unskillful regarding acceptance. Check in once in the morning (before noon), once in the afternoon (before 5:00 p.m.), and once in the evening. These should be short notes, allowing you to remember them for your evening review.

MORNING CHECK-IN

Skillful: _____

Unskillful: _____

AFTERNOON CHECK-IN

Skillful: _____

Unskillful: _____

EVENING CHECK-IN

Skillful: _____

Unskillful: _____

EVENING REVIEW

Reflecting on your day, what did you learn?

_____

_____

What was helpful about acceptance today?

_____

_____

What was difficult about acceptance today?

_____

_____

What did you do well today?

_____

_____

How can you make amends for, or improve upon, the unskillful actions of today?

_____

_____

WISDOM EXERCISE ONE, DAY SIX   **DATE:**

Morning Prayers and/or Reflection

MORNING REFLECTION

- You have a life of recovery filled with support and opportunities. Every day is a new opportunity and fresh start if you choose to take advantage of it.

- Remember that you are not the center of the universe but a valuable part of it. The events that happen in your life, whether you label them good or bad, are all opportunities to grow, learn, and make your life more meaningful.

- Bring to mind people and things you are grateful for. Make them relevant and personal.

- Take some time to reflect on the person you want to be. Set your intention to not waste this day and live it with attention and intention, cultivating the qualities that you find meaningful. Remember, the only thing that separates the person you are from the person you want to be is the action you take. Make a clear and firm commitment to your recovery today. You deserve to live a life free of addiction.

MORNING MEDITATION

Did you do it? _____   How long? _____

Set a clear intention and do your best to cultivate wise acceptance. Take an optimistic, problem-solving attitude. When you notice resistance or if things do not go your way, instead of dwelling on how something should have been different, see if you can move into acceptance and improve the situation. See how effectively you can learn to live in the real world, accepting life on life's terms, and see what lessons this has to offer you.

Check in three times a day, noting what actions were skillful and unskillful regarding acceptance. Check in once in the morning (before noon), once in the afternoon (before 5:00 p.m.), and once in the evening. These should be short notes, allowing you to remember them for your evening review.

MORNING CHECK-IN

Skillful: _____

Unskillful: _____

AFTERNOON CHECK-IN

Skillful: _____

Unskillful: _____

EVENING CHECK-IN

Skillful: _____

Unskillful: _____

EVENING REVIEW

Reflecting on your day, what did you learn?

_____

_____

What was helpful about acceptance today?

_____

_____

What was difficult about acceptance today?

_____

_____

What did you do well today?

_____

_____

How can you make amends for, or improve upon, the unskillful actions of today?

_____

_____

WISDOM EXERCISE ONE, DAY SEVEN   **DATE:**

Morning Prayers and/or Reflection

MORNING REFLECTION

- You have a life of recovery filled with support and opportunities. Every day is a new opportunity and fresh start if you choose to take advantage of it.

- Remember that you are not the center of the universe but a valuable part of it. The events that happen in your life, whether you label them good or bad, are all opportunities to grow, learn, and make your life more meaningful.

- Bring to mind people and things you are grateful for. Make them relevant and personal.

- Take some time to reflect on the person you want to be. Set your intention to not waste this day and live it with attention and intention, cultivating the qualities that you find meaningful. Remember, the only thing that separates the person you are from the person you want to be is the action you take. Make a clear and firm commitment to your recovery today. You deserve to live a life free of addiction.

MORNING MEDITATION

Did you do it? _____   How long? _____

Set a clear intention and do your best to cultivate wise acceptance. Take an optimistic, problem-solving attitude. When you notice resistance or if things do not go your way, instead of dwelling on how something should have been different, see if you can move into acceptance and improve the situation. See how effectively you can learn to live in the real world, accepting life on life's terms, and see what lessons this has to offer you.

Check in three times a day, noting what actions were skillful and unskillful regarding acceptance. Check in once in the morning (before noon), once in the afternoon (before 5:00 p.m.), and once in the evening. These should be short notes, allowing you to remember them for your evening review.

MORNING CHECK-IN

Skillful: _____

Unskillful: _____

AFTERNOON CHECK-IN

Skillful: _____

Unskillful: _____

EVENING CHECK-IN

Skillful: _____

Unskillful: _____

EVENING REVIEW

Reflecting on your day, what did you learn?

_____

_____

What was helpful about acceptance today?

_____

_____

What was difficult about acceptance today?

_____

_____

What did you do well today?

_____

_____

How can you make amends for, or improve upon, the unskillful actions of today?

_____

_____

WISDOM REVIEW

What were the most valuable lessons you learned this week?

_____

_____

_____

What were some of the ways you were able to benefit from acceptance?

_____

_____

_____

What did you do well this week that supports your recovery?

_____

_____

_____

What would you like to improve?

_____

_____

_____

EQUANIMITY

Developing the skill of equanimity will improve your ability to make truly healthy decisions in your life that support the person you want to be. It is an anchor to reality and rational thinking.

Equanimity is often described as a mind of calm or composure. It is a balanced state of mind that does not get caught up in extremes. It allows us to be present and stable even in difficult and challenging situations, not getting entangled in and identified with overpowering emotions, impulses, or desires.

Another way of describing equanimity is wise acceptance. As you no doubt discovered during your reflections on acceptance, many of your projections about how things ought to be, or how good or bad things could have been, did not necessarily hold up. With equanimity, we can recognize the value and opportunities in our lives without exaggeration. We can develop the ability to be wisely present with and accept whatever arises in each moment.

To be wisely present means to be aware of projections, elaborations, feelings, and attachments that may be limiting our ability to accept and see clearly what is happening. Again, accepting what is happening does not mean that we like it or are unwilling to change it. It means we understand that it is happening and there is a reason for it. It is neither all good nor all bad, and whether it is pleasant or unpleasant, we have the opportunity to respond to and engage with it in a way that is beneficial and healthy.

Through the cultivation of equanimity, we learn to engage with equal attention and care in all our experiences, including interactions with people we like, those we don't like, and strangers.

While this may sound difficult to achieve, every day we can make progress in cultivating a mind that is balanced, clear, and does not get caught up in exaggerations. You may notice that when you are calm, it is much easier to make decisions and choices that are healthy for you. However, when we are challenged or caught up in emotions such as sadness, fear, anger, or even happiness, it can become difficult to bring that same clarity of mind to our decisions. One of the keys to cultivating equanimity is to start noticing how we exaggerate the good and bad qualities in people, events, and simple activities in our lives.

Equanimity Exercise One

"Success is to be measured not so much by the position that one has reached in life as by the obstacles which he has overcome."

BOOKER T. WASHINGTON

It is interesting how we can find ourselves impressed by, or even enamored with, wealthy or famous people, such as musicians or movie stars, without actually knowing anything about their inner qualities or how they treat others. At the same time, we may not give much attention to, let alone have admiration for, the single parent raising children while working a couple of jobs or the elderly volunteer at the hospital dedicating time to ease people's suffering. We are all surrounded by amazing people of character who have daily obstacles to overcome merely to survive, as well as people who selflessly work to make the world a kinder place. In recovery, we usually get the honor of calling many of them friends.

While, upon reflection, we may decide these seemingly ordinary people of strong character and kindness are more deserving of our admiration, in our daily lives our attention and admiration is often drawn to those with a more glamorous lifestyle. This is not to say that those with glamorous lifestyles don't struggle or are not kind people worthy of admiration for both may be true. It is to say that our admiration is often directed at their lifestyle and position rather than their inner qualities.

When we look at our own lives, the accomplishments and things that required hard work are usually more deeply valued than those that came easily to us. We also value most the friends who have shared their struggles with us and allowed us to share ours with them. Booker T. Washington's quote reminds us that the path we traveled more accurately measures our growth and success than our destination does. With equanimity, we learn that traveling the bumpy roads can sometimes offer more to our journey than simply sticking to the smooth highways.

For the next two days, look for and identify the admirable qualities in the people you come into contact with. Take some time, as you are able, to bring some mindful attention to them and try to recognize at least one admirable quality about them.

EQUANIMITY EXERCISE ONE, DAY ONE   DATE:

Morning Prayers and/or Reflection

MORNING REFLECTION

- You have a life of recovery filled with support and opportunities. Every day is a new opportunity and fresh start if you choose to take advantage of it.

- Remember that you are not the center of the universe but a valuable part of it. The events that happen in your life, whether you label them good or bad, are all opportunities to grow, learn, and make your life more meaningful.

- Bring to mind people and things you are grateful for. Make them relevant and personal.

- Take some time to reflect on the person you want to be. Set your intention to not waste this day and live it with attention and intention, cultivating the qualities that you find meaningful. Remember, the only thing that separates the person you are from the person you want to be is the action you take. Make a clear and firm commitment to your recovery today. You deserve to live a life free of addiction.

MORNING MEDITATION

Did you do it? _____   How long? _____

Set a clear intention and do your best to notice the good qualities in others. Try to notice when you are focusing on people in negative ways and see if you can change your perspective.

Check in three times a day, noting what actions were skillful and unskillful regarding how you see others. Check in once in the morning (before noon), once in the afternoon (before 5:00 p.m.), and once in the evening. These should be short notes, allowing you to remember them for your evening review.

MORNING CHECK-IN

Skillful: _____

Unskillful: _____

AFTERNOON CHECK-IN

Skillful: _____

Unskillful: _____

EVENING CHECK-IN

Skillful: _____

Unskillful: _____

EVENING REVIEW

Reflecting on your day, what did you learn?

_____

_____

What were some of the qualities you noticed in others today?

_____

_____

How did noticing good qualities in others affect you?

_____

_____

What was difficult about seeing good qualities in others? Explain.

_____

_____

What did you do well today?

_____

_____

How can you make amends for, or improve upon, the unskillful actions of today?

_____

_____

EQUANIMITY EXERCISE ONE, DAY TWO   **DATE:**

Morning Prayers and/or Reflection

MORNING REFLECTION

- You have a life of recovery filled with support and opportunities. Every day is a new opportunity and fresh start if you choose to take advantage of it.

- Remember that you are not the center of the universe but a valuable part of it. The events that happen in your life, whether you label them good or bad, are all opportunities to grow, learn, and make your life more meaningful.

- Bring to mind people and things you are grateful for. Make them relevant and personal.

- Take some time to reflect on the person you want to be. Set your intention to not waste this day and live it with attention and intention, cultivating the qualities that you find meaningful. Remember, the only thing that separates the person you are from the person you want to be is the action you take. Make a clear and firm commitment to your recovery today. You deserve to live a life free of addiction.

MORNING MEDITATION

Did you do it? _____   How long? _____

Set a clear intention and do your best to notice the good qualities in others. Try to notice when you are focusing on people in negative ways and see if you can change your perspective.

Check in three times a day, noting what actions were skillful and unskillful regarding how you see others. Check in once in the morning (before noon), once in the afternoon (before 5:00 p.m.), and once in the evening. These should be short notes, allowing you to remember them for your evening review.

MORNING CHECK-IN

Skillful: _____

Unskillful: _____

AFTERNOON CHECK-IN

Skillful: _____

Unskillful: _____

EVENING CHECK-IN

Skillful: _____

Unskillful: _____

EVENING REVIEW

Reflecting on your day, what did you learn?

_____

_____

What were some of the qualities you noticed in others today?

_____

_____

How did noticing good qualities in others affect you?

_____

_____

What was difficult about seeing good qualities in others? Explain.

_____

_____

What did you do well today?

_____

_____

How can you make amends for, or improve upon, the unskillful actions of today?

_____

_____

Equanimity Exercise Two

"Expecting is the greatest impediment to living.
In anticipation of tomorrow, it loses today."

SENECA

Expectations, as we all know, play a huge role in our lives. We have all experienced disappointment and even despair because of expectations. Disappointment can arise when expectations are unmet, and despair can overtake us as we expect the worst to happen. We have also all experienced the joy of having things turn out beyond our expectations. On a subtler note, our expectations about situations or people can determine how we experience them. If we expect it to be a tough day at work, it usually is. If someone tells us that we will enjoy a restaurant, we usually do. Though this is not always the case, it is a common pattern and important to understand how our expectations create the attitudes we bring into our activities and interactions.

You may have heard this advice: just live your life without expectations and enjoy what happens. Though it sounds quite pleasant, this is untenable. There is no way we could function without expectations. When we go to the grocery store, we expect there to be groceries. When we attend our courses at college, we expect our teachers to be there. If we do our coursework, we expect to get a degree. If it's snowing outside, we expect it to be cold. When we go to the gas station, we expect it to be where it was the last time. As you can see, expectations have a role in our lives and are necessary for us to function.

Many expectations are not problematic; it is our unrealistic expectations that tend to get us into trouble. Unfortunately, when we investigate, we will probably find that we have many unrealistic expectations that need work. Most of us operate and make decisions based on unrealistic expectations that we hold to be true. How many times in our active addiction did we think we could feel good about who we were while doing things that would cause us pitiful, incomprehensible demoralization?

Other examples of unrealistic expectations include the following: our partner will always make us happy and understand us; a good career will provide us with happiness and stability; and if we eat right and exercise, we will be healthy and live a long life. We can hold these unrealistic expectations even though we know that relationships have ups and downs and sometimes require hard work; careers can never offer complete stability, and even people with good jobs can experience stress, worry, and fear; and no matter how healthy our food is or how much we exercise, we can still get sick or die at a young age.

In truth, life is messy for everyone and has its highs and lows. No one is immune. Thinking that we should be immune is an unrealistic expectation bound to cause us to suffer a great deal. All of us in recovery know the messiness of life and the opportunities for growth it presents.

If we develop equanimity through mindfulness, we can become aware of our unrealistic expectations and how they influence our interactions with others. Instead of developing unrealistic expectations, we can remember that our genuine happiness is always a result of living meaningfully today. We can remember that today will never come again and, while tomorrow promises opportunities that may or may not happen, the time to improve our lives is always now. It is a realistic expectation to believe that if we live each day cultivating the qualities we find to be meaningful, our days will be meaningful and so will our future. While we don't have power over the events in our lives, we do have power over the way we respond to them in recovery.

For the next two days, note your expectations throughout the day. Try to observe which expectations seem realistic and healthy and which may be based on an unrealistic assessment of a situation or the future. Watch for results of these varying expectations.

EQUANIMITY EXERCISE TWO, DAY ONE   DATE:

Morning Prayers and/or Reflection

MORNING REFLECTION

- You have a life of recovery filled with support and opportunities. Every day is a new opportunity and fresh start if you choose to take advantage of it.

- Remember that you are not the center of the universe but a valuable part of it. The events that happen in your life, whether you label them good or bad, are all opportunities to grow, learn, and make your life more meaningful.

- Bring to mind people and things you are grateful for. Make them relevant and personal.

- Take some time to reflect on the person you want to be. Set your intention to not waste this day and live it with attention and intention, cultivating the qualities that you find meaningful. Remember, the only thing that separates the person you are from the person you want to be is the action you take. Make a clear and firm commitment to your recovery today. You deserve to live a life free of addiction.

MORNING MEDITATION

Did you do it? _____   How long? _____

Set a clear intention and do your best to notice your expectations throughout the day. Try to observe which expectations seem realistic and healthy and which may be based on an unrealistic assessment of a situation or the future. Watch for results of these varying expectations.

Check in three times a day, noting what actions were skillful and unskillful regarding expectations. Check in once in the morning (before noon), once in the afternoon (before 5:00 p.m.), and once in the evening. These should be short notes, allowing you to remember them for your evening review.

MORNING CHECK-IN

Skillful: _____

Unskillful: _____

AFTERNOON CHECK-IN

Skillful: _____

Unskillful: _____

EVENING CHECK-IN

Skillful: _____

Unskillful: _____

EVENING REVIEW

Reflecting on your day, what did you learn?

_____

_____

What were some of the realistic expectations you had today?

_____

_____

What were some of the unrealistic expectations you had today?

_____

_____

How were you able to shift from unrealistic to realistic expectations?

_____

_____

What did you do well today?

_____

_____

How can you make amends for, or improve upon, the unskillful actions of today?

_____

_____

EQUANIMITY EXERCISE TWO, DAY TWO   DATE:

Morning Prayers and/or Reflection

MORNING REFLECTION

- You have a life of recovery filled with support and opportunities. Every day is a new opportunity and fresh start if you choose to take advantage of it.

- Remember that you are not the center of the universe but a valuable part of it. The events that happen in your life, whether you label them good or bad, are all opportunities to grow, learn, and make your life more meaningful.

- Bring to mind people and things you are grateful for. Make them relevant and personal.

- Take some time to reflect on the person you want to be. Set your intention to not waste this day and live it with attention and intention, cultivating the qualities that you find meaningful. Remember, the only thing that separates the person you are from the person you want to be is the action you take. Make a clear and firm commitment to your recovery today. You deserve to live a life free of addiction.

MORNING MEDITATION

Did you do it? _____   How long? _____

Set a clear intention and do your best to notice your expectations throughout the day. Try to observe which expectations seem realistic and healthy and which may be based on an unrealistic assessment of a situation or the future. Watch for results of these varying expectations.

Check in three times a day, noting what actions were skillful and unskillful regarding expectations. Check in once in the morning (before noon), once in the afternoon (before 5:00 p.m.), and once in the evening. These should be short notes, allowing you to remember them for your evening review.

MORNING CHECK-IN

Skillful: _____

Unskillful: _____

AFTERNOON CHECK-IN

Skillful: _____

Unskillful: _____

EVENING CHECK-IN

Skillful: _____

Unskillful: _____

EVENING REVIEW

Reflecting on your day, what did you learn?

_____

_____

What were some of the realistic expectations you had today?

_____

_____

What were some of the unrealistic expectations you had today?

_____

_____

How were you able to shift from unrealistic to realistic expectations?

_____

_____

What did you do well today?

_____

_____

How can you make amends for, or improve upon, the unskillful actions of today?

_____

_____

Equanimity Exercise Three

_"Each time we drop our complaints and allow everyday good
fortune to inspire us, we enter the warrior's world."_

PEMA CHÖDRÖN

Equanimity allows us to avoid extremes and exaggerations. With equanimity, we can bring a piercing wisdom into our experiences without preconceptions, elaborations, or unrealistic expectations. In doing so, we are more able to recognize and take advantage of the opportunities our experiences present, making the best use of our lives. This does not mean we don't experience the pure joy of pleasurable activities or the pain of difficult ones. It means we understand that both are temporary and can only arise in dependence upon each other. For example, it is only through the struggle of adversity that we get to know the joy of accomplishment.

Cultivating equanimity in daily life is about learning to give equal attention to _all_ our activities, not just the ones we look forward to or the ones we are trying to avoid. When we reflect upon the things we give our attention to the most, we will find they are related to our attachments and our aversions. We spend a lot of time and energy focusing on the people and things we enjoy and avoiding the ones we don't. However, we spend the clear majority of our lives somewhere between enjoyment and avoidance and, as we reflected upon previously, in anticipation of future events, we often do not participate fully in the current moments of our lives.

Pema Chödrön's quote reminds us that our days in recovery are filled with incredible opportunities to embrace and grow. At any given moment, if we pause and look around, we can see much to be grateful for, be inspired by, and rejoice in—the water that gives us life, the relationships that nourish us, the people who support our recovery and have our best interests in mind, the food we have to eat, the creativity that solves problems and results in beauty, the compassion we have for others, and the kindness we share. At the end of our lives, we may find that time spent taking care of an ill friend was far more rewarding than attending the concert we missed.

Today drop your complaints and enter the warrior's world. Recognize the value of your current situation and all it has to offer. Remember that the only difference between an obstacle and an opportunity is the way you perceive it.

EQUANIMITY EXERCISE THREE   DATE:

Morning Prayers and/or Reflection

MORNING REFLECTION

- You have a life of recovery filled with support and opportunities. Every day is a new opportunity and fresh start if you choose to take advantage of it.

- Remember that you are not the center of the universe but a valuable part of it. The events that happen in your life, whether you label them good or bad, are all opportunities to grow, learn, and make your life more meaningful.

- Bring to mind people and things you are grateful for. Make them relevant and personal.

- Take some time to reflect on the person you want to be. Set your intention to not waste this day and live it with attention and intention, cultivating the qualities that you find meaningful. Remember, the only thing that separates the person you are from the person you want to be is the action you take. Make a clear and firm commitment to your recovery today. You deserve to live a life free of addiction.

MORNING MEDITATION

Did you do it? _____   How long? _____

Set a clear intention and do your best to avoid complaining. Adopt an attitude of gratitude and focus on problem solving today. Notice how this affects your attitude and interactions with others.

Check in three times a day, noting what actions were skillful and unskillful regarding your intention today. Check in once in the morning (before noon), once in the afternoon (before 5:00 p.m.), and once in the evening. These should be short notes, allowing you to remember them for your evening review.

MORNING CHECK-IN

Skillful: _____

Unskillful: _____

AFTERNOON CHECK-IN

Skillful: _____

Unskillful: _____

EVENING CHECK-IN

Skillful: _____

Unskillful: _____

EVENING REVIEW

Reflecting on your day, what did you learn?

_____

_____

What were some of the benefits of not complaining?

_____

_____

What was difficult about trying not to complain?

_____

_____

What did you do well today?

_____

_____

How can you make amends for, or improve upon, the unskillful actions of today?

_____

_____

Equanimity Exercise Four

*"What you see and hear . . .
depends on what kind of a person you are."*

C.S. LEWIS

Even though we may have learned it at some point in our lives, it is easy to forget that the world we experience is a subjective one. We tend to think there is an objective world out there and everyone else experiences it in the same way we do. We believe the food at our favorite restaurant is truly delicious, our favorite part of town is beautiful, and our friends are wonderful people. However, it would be more accurate to say we find the food at our favorite restaurant delicious, we find our favorite part of town beautiful, and we really enjoy our friends and find them wonderful. At the same time, others may not like our favorite restaurant, may not care for our favorite part of town, and may think even our best friends are not so wonderful.

We see the world through the lens of our personal experience, which is shaped by the environment in which we were raised, our culture, our belief system, and our values. Those raised in other environments and cultures, or with belief systems other than our own, can experience the same people, places, and activities differently, for example, people from different political parties are apt to have different opinions of a particular candidate. The key point here is that, while our perceptions, opinions, and views seem to make perfect sense to us, the different perceptions, opinions, and views of others make perfect sense to them. If we reflect on our life, we will see that our own views and beliefs have changed over time. If we remember this, it can help us stay away from extreme views and have a broader perspective—as well as an inclusive attitude—in our interactions with others.

When we are in a good mood and feeling healthy and happy, people we usually find annoying don't seem to bother us as much. When we are tired, irritable, or not feeling well, we can feel annoyed even by our best friends. Our attitude and our mental and emotional state play a large part in how we experience others and the activities we engage in. C.S. Lewis's quote reminds us of the simple truth we are usually not conscious of: we are just one of many humans sharing this planet, each of us experiencing it through our unique lens, a lens that can change from moment to moment and from day to day. In recovery, we learn that as we change our perspective or attitude we also change our experience of the world.

For the next two days, explore the subjective experience of your daily activities. Explore the idea that things can change if you change your attitude or perspective about them. Notice how others experience things differently than you do. When talking to others, do your best to remember that, even if their opinions are different from yours, those opinions are valid from their point of view.

EQUANIMITY EXERCISE FOUR, DAY ONE DATE:

Morning Prayers and/or Reflection

MORNING REFLECTION

- You have a life of recovery filled with support and opportunities. Every day is a new opportunity and fresh start if you choose to take advantage of it.

- Remember that you are not the center of the universe but a valuable part of it. The events that happen in your life, whether you label them good or bad, are all opportunities to grow, learn, and make your life more meaningful.

- Bring to mind people and things you are grateful for. Make them relevant and personal.

- Take some time to reflect on the person you want to be. Set your intention to not waste this day and live it with attention and intention, cultivating the qualities that you find meaningful. Remember, the only thing that separates the person you are from the person you want to be is the action you take. Make a clear and firm commitment to your recovery today. You deserve to live a life free of addiction.

MORNING MEDITATION

Did you do it? _____   How long? _____

Set a clear intention and do your best to explore the idea that things can change if you alter your attitude or perspective about them. Notice how others experience things differently than you do. When talking to others, do your best to remember that even if people's opinions are different from yours, their opinions are valid from their point of view.

Check in three times a day, noting what actions were skillful and unskillful regarding your attitude. Check in once in the morning (before noon), once in the afternoon (before 5:00 p.m.), and once in the evening. These should be short notes, allowing you to remember them for your evening review.

MORNING CHECK-IN

Skillful: _____

Unskillful: _____

AFTERNOON CHECK-IN

Skillful: _____

Unskillful: _____

EVENING CHECK-IN

Skillful: _____

Unskillful: _____

EVENING REVIEW

Reflecting on your day, what did you learn?

_____

_____

In what ways was it beneficial to change your attitude or perspective?

_____

_____

In what ways was it difficult to change your attitude or perspective?

_____

_____

What did you do well today?

_____

_____

How can you make amends for, or improve upon, the unskillful actions of today?

_____

_____

EQUANIMITY EXERCISE FOUR, DAY TWO   DATE:

Morning Prayers and/or Reflection

MORNING REFLECTION

- You have a life of recovery filled with support and opportunities. Every day is a new opportunity and fresh start if you choose to take advantage of it.

- Remember that you are not the center of the universe but a valuable part of it. The events that happen in your life, whether you label them good or bad, are all opportunities to grow, learn, and make your life more meaningful.

- Bring to mind people and things you are grateful for. Make them relevant and personal.

- Take some time to reflect on the person you want to be. Set your intention to not waste this day and live it with attention and intention, cultivating the qualities that you find meaningful. Remember, the only thing that separates the person you are from the person you want to be is the action you take. Make a clear and firm commitment to your recovery today. You deserve to live a life free of addiction.

MORNING MEDITATION

Did you do it? _____   How long? _____

Set a clear intention and do your best to explore the idea that things can change if you alter your attitude or perspective about them. Notice how others experience things differently than you do. When talking to others, do your best to remember that even if people's opinions are different from yours, their opinions are valid from their point of view.

Check in three times a day, noting what actions were skillful and unskillful regarding your attitude. Check in once in the morning (before noon), once in the afternoon (before 5:00 p.m.), and once in the evening. These should be short notes, allowing you to remember them for your evening review.

MORNING CHECK-IN

Skillful: _____

Unskillful: _____

AFTERNOON CHECK-IN

Skillful: _____

Unskillful: _____

EVENING CHECK-IN

Skillful: _____

Unskillful: _____

EVENING REVIEW

Reflecting on your day, what did you learn?

_____

_____

In what ways was it beneficial to change your attitude or perspective?

_____

_____

In what ways was it difficult to change your attitude or perspective?

_____

_____

What did you do well today?

_____

_____

How can you make amends for, or improve upon, the unskillful actions of today?

_____

_____

EQUANIMITY EXERCISE FOUR, DAY THREE   DATE:

Morning Prayers and/or Reflection

MORNING REFLECTION

- You have a life of recovery filled with support and opportunities. Every day is a new opportunity and fresh start if you choose to take advantage of it.

- Remember that you are not the center of the universe but a valuable part of it. The events that happen in your life, whether you label them good or bad, are all opportunities to grow, learn, and make your life more meaningful.

- Bring to mind people and things you are grateful for. Make them relevant and personal.

- Take some time to reflect on the person you want to be. Set your intention to not waste this day and live it with attention and intention, cultivating the qualities that you find meaningful. Remember, the only thing that separates the person you are from the person you want to be is the action you take. Make a clear and firm commitment to your recovery today. You deserve to live a life free of addiction.

MORNING MEDITATION

Did you do it? _____   How long? _____

Set a clear intention and do your best to explore the idea that things can change if you alter your attitude or perspective about them. Notice how others experience things differently than you do. When talking to others, do your best to remember that even if people's opinions are different from yours, their opinions are valid from their point of view.

Check in three times a day, noting what actions were skillful and unskillful regarding your attitude. Check in once in the morning (before noon), once in the afternoon (before 5:00 p.m.), and once in the evening. These should be short notes, allowing you to remember them for your evening review.

MORNING CHECK-IN

Skillful: _____

Unskillful: _____

AFTERNOON CHECK-IN

Skillful: _____

Unskillful: _____

EVENING CHECK-IN

Skillful: _____

Unskillful: _____

EVENING REVIEW

Reflecting on your day, what did you learn?

_____

_____

In what ways was it beneficial to change your attitude or perspective?

_____

_____

In what ways was it difficult to change your attitude or perspective?

_____

_____

What did you do well today?

_____

_____

How can you make amends for, or improve upon, the unskillful actions of today?

_____

_____

EQUANIMITY REVIEW

What were the most valuable lessons you learned this week?

_____

_____

_____

What were some of the ways you exaggerated events, people, or your own feelings this week?

_____

_____

_____

What did you do well this week that supports your recovery?

_____

_____

_____

COMPASSION

Compassion is an incredibly powerful force that motivates us to address and confront the true sources of suffering in the lives of others as well as our own. It is the direct antidote to the harmful mental states of cruelty and ill will.

Often misunderstood by us, compassion is rarely fully developed in our lives. Some people have the idea that if they are compassionate they will feel sad all the time, which is a common confusion in our culture. Compassion does not lead to sadness. It is when we recognize the sadness and suffering of ourselves or others that compassion arises, making it the result of sadness and suffering, not the cause. Out of compassion, we can find the strength and wisdom to respond to life's challenges in healthy and productive ways that support our recovery.

Compassion is not simply the feeling of sadness that arises when we see suffering. It is the heartfelt desire, triggered by sadness, to eliminate suffering. The suffering we endure when our lives are run by addiction offers one positive opportunity—the opportunity to develop deep compassion for others. In recovery, we often first experience compassion by being on the receiving end of it. The wisdom of compassion is the ability to make healthy choices and engage in actions that remove or reduce suffering in ourselves and others.

Cultivating the power of compassion starts with developing a meaningful connection with others, which increases our ability to be empathetic as well as receive the empathy of others. Empathy allows us to relate to and understand the suffering of others and leads to compassion—the desire to help remove the suffering. Compassion is one of the most powerful qualities we can cultivate. It becomes the motivation that inspires us to develop skillful methods and wholesome life habits to eliminate suffering.

Compassion Exercise One

"The best way to find yourself is to lose yourself in the service of others."

MAHATMA GANDHI

One of the benefits of cultivating empathy and compassion in our recovery is that it expands our understanding of ourselves and connects us to our world. Ultimately, we know the world only through the lens of our personal experience. We are the center of our universe when it comes to personal knowledge and the experience of it. Of course, this is a limited understanding because each of us is only one of more than seven billion humans on this planet, all with their own personal experiences, ideas, values, and understanding of the world. Unfortunately, it is easy to forget we have such a limited perspective and, unless we actively seek to expand it, we can lose our opportunity to discover our own inner resources and meaning in life.

If we are to know ourselves deeply, it is essential that we explore our connection with others and experience life through a wide variety of perspectives and experiences. It is difficult to learn much about ourselves and what is truly meaningful in life if we remain focused primarily on our own needs. In fact, not only do we miss the opportunity to grow in more meaningful ways, but we also suffer more. One of the great paradoxes is that the more we focus on ourselves the more we are troubled by even small things that don't go our way. Conversely, as we become more we-centered instead of me-centered, not only do we find more meaning and purpose in life, but also many of the self-centered problems that once plagued us give way to a deeper sense of self-worth and well-being.

As Mahatma Gandhi points out, one of the best ways to discover ourselves, including our own value and potential, is to be helpful to others in need. In helping others, we see and experience firsthand struggle, resiliency, character, success, and failure. These are all seeds of our own personal development and inner wisdom.

For the next two days, find ways to be of service to others. It would be ideal to be helpful to people different from you in some way or simply someone you find challenging to be around. Let your motivation be that of compassion, desiring to help lighten their suffering in some way.

COMPASSION EXERCISE ONE, DAY ONE   DATE:

Morning Prayers and/or Reflection

MORNING REFLECTION

- You have a life of recovery filled with support and opportunities. Every day is a new opportunity and fresh start if you choose to take advantage of it.

- Remember that you are not the center of the universe but a valuable part of it. The events that happen in your life, whether you label them good or bad, are all opportunities to grow, learn, and make your life more meaningful.

- Bring to mind people and things you are grateful for. Make them relevant and personal.

- Take some time to reflect on the person you want to be. Set your intention to not waste this day and live it with attention and intention, cultivating the qualities that you find meaningful. Remember, the only thing that separates the person you are from the person you want to be is the action you take. Make a clear and firm commitment to your recovery today. You deserve to live a life free of addiction.

MORNING MEDITATION

Did you do it? _____   How long? _____

Set a clear intention and do your best to be of service to others. It would be ideal to be helpful to people different from you in some way, or someone you find challenging to be around. Let your motivation be that of compassion, desiring to help lighten his or her suffering in some way.

Check in three times a day, noting what actions were skillful and unskillful regarding being helpful. Check in once in the morning (before noon), once in the afternoon (before 5:00 p.m.), and once in the evening. These should be short notes, allowing you to remember them for your evening review.

MORNING CHECK-IN

Skillful: _____

Unskillful: _____

AFTERNOON CHECK-IN

Skillful: _____

Unskillful: _____

EVENING CHECK-IN

Skillful: _____

Unskillful: _____

EVENING REVIEW

Reflecting on your day, what did you learn?

_____

_____

In what ways was it beneficial to be helpful to others?

_____

_____

In what ways was it difficult to be helpful to others?

_____

_____

What did you do well today?

_____

_____

How can you make amends for, or improve upon, the unskillful actions of today?

_____

_____

COMPASSION EXERCISE ONE, DAY TWO   **DATE:**

Morning Prayers and/or Reflection

MORNING REFLECTION

- You have a life of recovery filled with support and opportunities. Every day is a new opportunity and fresh start if you choose to take advantage of it.

- Remember that you are not the center of the universe but a valuable part of it. The events that happen in your life, whether you label them good or bad, are all opportunities to grow, learn, and make your life more meaningful.

- Bring to mind people and things you are grateful for. Make them relevant and personal.

- Take some time to reflect on the person you want to be. Set your intention to not waste this day and live it with attention and intention, cultivating the qualities that you find meaningful. Remember, the only thing that separates the person you are from the person you want to be is the action you take. Make a clear and firm commitment to your recovery today. You deserve to live a life free of addiction.

MORNING MEDITATION

Did you do it? _____   How long? _____

Set a clear intention and do your best to be of service to others. It would be ideal to be helpful to people different from you in some way, or someone you find challenging to be around. Let your motivation be that of compassion, desiring to help lighten his or her suffering in some way.

Check in three times a day, noting what actions were skillful and unskillful regarding being helpful. Check in once in the morning (before noon), once in the afternoon (before 5:00 p.m.), and once in the evening. These should be short notes, allowing you to remember them for your evening review.

MORNING CHECK-IN

Skillful: _____

Unskillful: _____

AFTERNOON CHECK-IN

Skillful: _____

Unskillful: _____

EVENING CHECK-IN

Skillful: _____

Unskillful: _____

EVENING REVIEW

Reflecting on your day, what did you learn?

_____

_____

In what ways was it beneficial to be helpful to others?

_____

_____

In what ways was it difficult to be helpful to others?

_____

_____

What did you do well today?

_____

_____

How can you make amends for, or improve upon, the unskillful actions of today?

_____

_____

Compassion Exercise Two

*"Compassion doesn't, of course,
mean feeling sorry for people, or pity."*

KAREN ARMSTRONG

Those of us in recovery are all too familiar with words and phrases such as *pity* and *feeling less than*. Pity is often confused with compassion. In our common usage of the words and in our dictionaries, *pity* and *compassion* can become interchangeable synonyms. However, when we are cultivating the transformative power of compassion within our mindfulness practice, compassion is clearly different from pity or feeling sorry for someone. It is an active state in which we desire to remove someone's suffering whenever possible—a state that arises from the recognition of our shared humanity and the intrinsic value we all have.

In its truest form, compassion is a relationship of equals. We rarely have pity for those we see as equals, and feeling sorrow for others is not the same as the desire to remove their suffering. If we look closely, we can see how much more powerful compassion can be in transforming both our lives and the world we live in, much more so than pity or sorrow. For us to find recovery, others, instead of looking down on us, showed us our value as equals. Now we have the opportunity to do the same for others.

To cultivate compassion in this way, it is important to develop empathy and recognize the value of others and our connection to them. One excellent method is to recite and reflect upon the following verse throughout the day.

Just like me, all others are trying to find happiness.

Just like me, all others are trying to avoid suffering.

Just like me, all others have known sadness, despair, and loss.

Just like me, all others are trying to get their needs met.

Just like me, all others are learning how to live.

Just like me, all others are deserving of compassion.

For the next two days, recite and reflect upon this verse throughout your day and be as compassionate as you can with yourself and others. There is also a guided meditation, titled "Just Like Me," based on this verse that you may find useful in the Mindful Life Community.

COMPASSION EXERCISE TWO, DAY ONE   **DATE:**

Morning Prayers and/or Reflection

MORNING REFLECTION

- You have a life of recovery filled with support and opportunities. Every day is a new opportunity and fresh start if you choose to take advantage of it.

- Remember that you are not the center of the universe but a valuable part of it. The events that happen in your life, whether you label them good or bad, are all opportunities to grow, learn, and make your life more meaningful.

- Bring to mind people and things you are grateful for. Make them relevant and personal.

- Take some time to reflect on the person you want to be. Set your intention to not waste this day and live it with attention and intention, cultivating the qualities that you find meaningful. Remember, the only thing that separates the person you are from the person you want to be is the action you take. Make a clear and firm commitment to your recovery today. You deserve to live a life free of addiction.

MORNING MEDITATION

Did you do it? _____ How long? _____

Set a clear intention and do your best to recite and reflect upon the "Just Like Me" verses throughout your day and be as compassionate as you can with yourself and others.

Check in three times a day, noting what actions were skillful and unskillful regarding having compassion for others. Check in once in the morning (before noon), once in the afternoon (before 5:00 p.m.), and once in the evening. These should be short notes, allowing you to remember them for your evening review.

MORNING CHECK-IN

Skillful: _____

Unskillful: _____

AFTERNOON CHECK-IN

Skillful: _____

Unskillful: _____

EVENING CHECK-IN

Skillful: _____

Unskillful: _____

EVENING REVIEW

Reflecting on your day, what did you learn?

_____

_____

In what ways was it beneficial to reflect on the verses?

_____

_____

In what ways was it difficult to bring the verses to mind?

_____

_____

What did you do well today?

_____

_____

How can you make amends for, or improve upon, the unskillful actions of today?

_____

_____

COMPASSION EXERCISE TWO, DAY TWO   DATE:

Morning Prayers and/or Reflection

MORNING REFLECTION

- You have a life of recovery filled with support and opportunities. Every day is a new opportunity and fresh start if you choose to take advantage of it.

- Remember that you are not the center of the universe but a valuable part of it. The events that happen in your life, whether you label them good or bad, are all opportunities to grow, learn, and make your life more meaningful.

- Bring to mind people and things you are grateful for. Make them relevant and personal.

- Take some time to reflect on the person you want to be. Set your intention to not waste this day and live it with attention and intention, cultivating the qualities that you find meaningful. Remember, the only thing that separates the person you are from the person you want to be is the action you take. Make a clear and firm commitment to your recovery today. You deserve to live a life free of addiction.

MORNING MEDITATION

Did you do it? _____   How long? _____

Set a clear intention and do your best to recite and reflect upon the "Just Like Me" verses throughout your day and be as compassionate as you can with yourself and others.

Check in three times a day, noting what actions were skillful and unskillful regarding having compassion for others. Check in once in the morning (before noon), once in the afternoon (before 5:00 p.m.), and once in the evening. These should be short notes, allowing you to remember them for your evening review.

MORNING CHECK-IN

Skillful: _____

Unskillful: _____

AFTERNOON CHECK-IN

Skillful: _____

Unskillful: _____

EVENING CHECK-IN

Skillful: _____

Unskillful: _____

EVENING REVIEW

Reflecting on your day, what did you learn?

_____

_____

In what ways was it beneficial to reflect on the verses?

_____

_____

In what ways was it difficult to bring the verses to mind?

_____

_____

What did you do well today?

_____

_____

How can you make amends for, or improve upon, the unskillful actions of today?

_____

_____

Compassion Exercise Three

"All the world is full of suffering. It is also full of overcoming."

HELEN KELLER

What we are paying attention to in any given moment becomes important to us. The more attention we give it the more significant it becomes, overriding our attention to other things. Just as this was true in our times of active addiction, it is true in our recovery. If we are thinking about an upcoming vacation, it brings anticipation and takes us away from our current situation. If we are worrying about something, it brings anxiety and takes us away from the present moment, one in which there may not be anything to worry about.

The more attention we give a thought the more influence that thought has on our mind. When our attention is focused on something, our awareness is limited to those thoughts. When we are anticipating our upcoming vacation, it is difficult to recognize the joys that are right in front of us. When we are caught up in worry, it is difficult to be aware of all we have to be grateful for in this moment. Understanding this, it is important to remember that whatever we are focusing on is never the whole picture and we can develop the ability to redirect our attention, allowing us to gain perspective and cultivate healthier and more beneficial attitudes as we engage in our day.

Sometimes we can become overwhelmed by our personal suffering or the suffering we see in the world. The more attention we give the suffering the more hopeless we can feel. We can fall into unproductive attitudes and habits, such as blame, apathy, despair, or anger. As Helen Keller's quote points out, the world is full of suffering. In fact, everyone you will ever meet has had their share of suffering and will continue to have more. We have also all had healing, joy, and deep connections formed by the shared experience of overcoming struggles and hardships. It is out of compassion that we have found our recovery. We would not be here now, with this precious opportunity, without the suffering that brought us here. Recovery is an act of compassion for ourselves and others.

It is important to identify suffering and empathize with others. How else can we overcome it? However, if we focus only on the suffering, believing we are simply victims of it, we cannot see the compassion all around us. This compassion is what empowers us to overcome suffering. With compassion, we recognize and understand that all of us have challenges and tragedies throughout our lives. We also have joys, opportunities, and resources that far outnumber the challenges and tragedies. Compassion does not allow or ignore suffering, nor does it allow us to let the suffering we encounter overshadow the overwhelming goodness and strength in all of us. If we direct our attention beyond the difficult moments we are attending to, we can find the inspiration and strength to overcome them. In this way, compassion is a vital supplement that fuels our recovery.

For the next two days, direct your attention toward all the compassion you see. Try to notice how you and others help alleviate suffering, even in the smallest of ways.

COMPASSION EXERCISE THREE, DAY ONE   DATE:

Morning Prayers and/or Reflection

MORNING REFLECTION

- You have a life of recovery filled with support and opportunities. Every day is a new opportunity and fresh start if you choose to take advantage of it.

- Remember that you are not the center of the universe but a valuable part of it. The events that happen in your life, whether you label them good or bad, are all opportunities to grow, learn, and make your life more meaningful.

- Bring to mind people and things you are grateful for. Make them relevant and personal.

- Take some time to reflect on the person you want to be. Set your intention to not waste this day and live it with attention and intention, cultivating the qualities that you find meaningful. Remember, the only thing that separates the person you are from the person you want to be is the action you take. Make a clear and firm commitment to your recovery today. You deserve to live a life free of addiction.

MORNING MEDITATION

Did you do it? _____   How long? _____

Set a clear intention and do your best to direct your attention to all the compassion you see. Try to notice how you and others help alleviate suffering, even in the smallest of ways.

Check in three times a day, noting what actions were skillful and unskillful regarding having compassion for others. Check in once in the morning (before noon), once in the afternoon (before 5:00 p.m.), and once in the evening. These should be short notes, allowing you to remember them for your evening review.

MORNING CHECK-IN

Skillful: _____

Unskillful: _____

AFTERNOON CHECK-IN

Skillful: _____

Unskillful: _____

EVENING CHECK-IN

Skillful: _____

Unskillful: _____

EVENING REVIEW

Reflecting on your day, what did you learn?

_____

_____

In what ways was it beneficial to notice compassion?

_____

_____

In what ways was it beneficial to act compassionately?

_____

_____

What was challenging about this exercise?

_____

_____

What did you do well today?

_____

_____

How can you make amends for, or improve upon, the unskillful actions of today?

_____

_____

COMPASSION EXERCISE THREE, DAY TWO   DATE:

Morning Prayers and/or Reflection

MORNING REFLECTION

- You have a life of recovery filled with support and opportunities. Every day is a new opportunity and fresh start if you choose to take advantage of it.

- Remember that you are not the center of the universe but a valuable part of it. The events that happen in your life, whether you label them good or bad, are all opportunities to grow, learn, and make your life more meaningful.

- Bring to mind people and things you are grateful for. Make them relevant and personal.

- Take some time to reflect on the person you want to be. Set your intention to not waste this day and live it with attention and intention, cultivating the qualities that you find meaningful. Remember, the only thing that separates the person you are from the person you want to be is the action you take. Make a clear and firm commitment to your recovery today. You deserve to live a life free of addiction.

MORNING MEDITATION

Did you do it? _____ How long? _____

Set a clear intention and do your best to direct your attention to all the compassion you see. Try to notice how you and others help alleviate suffering, even in the smallest of ways.

Check in three times a day, noting what actions were skillful and unskillful regarding having compassion for others. Check in once in the morning (before noon), once in the afternoon (before 5:00 p.m.), and once in the evening. These should be short notes, allowing you to remember them for your evening review.

MORNING CHECK-IN

Skillful: _____

Unskillful: _____

AFTERNOON CHECK-IN

Skillful: _____

Unskillful: _____

EVENING CHECK-IN

Skillful: _____

Unskillful: _____

EVENING REVIEW

Reflecting on your day, what did you learn?

_____

_____

In what ways was it beneficial to notice compassion?

_____

_____

In what ways was it beneficial to act compassionately?

_____

_____

What was challenging about this exercise?

_____

_____

What did you do well today?

_____

_____

How can you make amends for, or improve upon, the unskillful actions of today?

_____

_____

Compassion Exercise Four

"When we forgive others, we give ourselves
permission to let go of our own suffering."

JOHN BRUNA

One of the most powerful forms of compassion is forgiveness. If we are to really flourish in our recovery, it is essential that we learn to forgive ourselves and others. Holding onto old pains, resentments, and ill will toward others can only bring us suffering. Even now, if we reflect upon an old injustice done to us, anger, agitation, or some other form of pain can arise within us. Wishing ill upon others, as the old saying goes, is like squeezing a hot coal in our own hand hoping someone else will feel the pain. In the end, not only does ill will not change the past, but it also continues to harm us in the present.

On the other hand, while forgiveness does not change the past, it does empower us to heal and increases the ability to develop healthier relationships. When we forgive someone, it sometimes seems like we are doing them a big favor. However, in truth, as the quote at the beginning of this section reminds us, we are essentially giving ourselves permission to let go of our own suffering and heal. Instead of watering the seeds of our own suffering with indignation and victimization, we can plant seeds of forgiveness and nourish them with compassion for ourselves and others. What kinder gift could we give ourselves than to allow ourselves to heal old wounds, letting go of pain we no longer need to feel?

To forgive, it is helpful to remember that all of us have made mistakes, harmed others, and done things we regret. This does not make us bad people. It simply reminds us that we are all still learning how to live with each other and find our way in this world. Likewise, we all have done many kind and wonderful things we feel good about. When we recall our own past mistakes and compassionately learn to forgive ourselves, it allows us to forgive others. In doing so, it is an act of compassion for all concerned.

Today work on forgiving others. If possible, call to mind some old resentments and see if it is time to let them go. Wish others well, knowing that the better off they are the better off we all are. Throughout your day, when you catch yourself getting irritated by others, do your best to let go of the agitation and recognize that they, just like you, are doing the best they can.

COMPASSION EXERCISE FOUR, DAY ONE   DATE:

Morning Prayers and/or Reflection

MORNING REFLECTION

- You have a life of recovery filled with support and opportunities. Every day is a new opportunity and fresh start if you choose to take advantage of it.

- Remember that you are not the center of the universe but a valuable part of it. The events that happen in your life, whether you label them good or bad, are all opportunities to grow, learn, and make your life more meaningful.

- Bring to mind people and things you are grateful for. Make them relevant and personal.

- Take some time to reflect on the person you want to be. Set your intention to not waste this day and live it with attention and intention, cultivating the qualities that you find meaningful. Remember, the only thing that separates the person you are from the person you want to be is the action you take. Make a clear and firm commitment to your recovery today. You deserve to live a life free of addiction.

MORNING MEDITATION

Did you do it? _____   How long? _____

Set a clear intention and do your best to forgive yourself and others. Call to mind some old resentments and see if it is time to let them go so you can heal. Throughout your day, when you do something you don't feel good about, forgive yourself and make a commitment to do better instead of being critical. When you catch yourself getting irritated by others, do your best to let go of the agitation and recognize that they, just like you, are doing the best they can.

Check in three times a day, noting what actions were skillful and unskillful regarding forgiveness. Check in once in the morning (before noon), once in the afternoon (before 5:00 p.m.), and once in the evening. These should be short notes, allowing you to remember them for your evening review.

MORNING CHECK-IN

Skillful: _____

Unskillful: _____

AFTERNOON CHECK-IN

Skillful: _____

Unskillful: _____

EVENING CHECK-IN

Skillful: _____

Unskillful: _____

EVENING REVIEW

Reflecting on your day, what did you learn?

_____

_____

Were you able to forgive anyone? Explain.

_____

_____

Were you able to be forgiving to yourself? Explain.

_____

_____

What was challenging about this exercise?

_____

_____

What did you do well today?

_____

_____

How can you make amends for, or improve upon, the unskillful actions of today?

_____

_____

COMPASSION EXERCISE FOUR, DAY TWO   DATE:

Morning Prayers and/or Reflection

MORNING REFLECTION

- You have a life of recovery filled with support and opportunities. Every day is a new opportunity and fresh start if you choose to take advantage of it.

- Remember that you are not the center of the universe but a valuable part of it. The events that happen in your life, whether you label them good or bad, are all opportunities to grow, learn, and make your life more meaningful.

- Bring to mind people and things you are grateful for. Make them relevant and personal.

- Take some time to reflect on the person you want to be. Set your intention to not waste this day and live it with attention and intention, cultivating the qualities that you find meaningful. Remember, the only thing that separates the person you are from the person you want to be is the action you take. Make a clear and firm commitment to your recovery today. You deserve to live a life free of addiction.

MORNING MEDITATION

Did you do it? _____   How long? _____

Set a clear intention and do your best to forgive yourself and others. Call to mind some old resentments and see if it is time to let them go so you can heal. Throughout your day, when you do something you don't feel good about, forgive yourself and make a commitment to do better instead of being critical. When you catch yourself getting irritated by others, do your best to let go of the agitation and recognize that they, just like you, are doing the best they can.

Check in three times a day, noting what actions were skillful and unskillful regarding forgiveness. Check in once in the morning (before noon), once in the afternoon (before 5:00 p.m.), and once in the evening. These should be short notes, allowing you to remember them for your evening review.

MORNING CHECK-IN

Skillful: _____

Unskillful: _____

AFTERNOON CHECK-IN

Skillful: _____

Unskillful: _____

EVENING CHECK-IN

Skillful: _____

Unskillful: _____

EVENING REVIEW

Reflecting on your day, what did you learn?

_____

_____

Were you able to forgive anyone? Explain.

_____

_____

Were you able to be forgiving to yourself? Explain.

_____

_____

What was challenging about this exercise?

_____

_____

What did you do well today?

_____

_____

How can you make amends for, or improve upon, the unskillful actions of today?

_____

_____

Compassion Exercise Five

"When compassion awakens in your heart,
you're able to be more honest with yourself."

MINGYUR RINPOCHE

We all know how difficult it can be to take a clear and discerning look at ourselves. We even call it "taking a hard look" at ourselves. We all have our defenses, insecurities, and fears that can prevent us from looking inward. Our pride, which attempts to mask our deeper insecurities, can rationalize behaviors and habits that prevent us from being authentic with ourselves and others. On the other side of the coin, we can be too hard on ourselves, beating ourselves up for mistakes and behaviors that don't live up to some ideal of how we think we should be. The task of becoming self-reflective in an accurate and nurturing way is not easy, but it is critical for our recovery and requires compassion and practice.

If we can learn to be compassionate with ourselves and others, we will become more accepting and supportive. This provides us with the opportunity to let our walls fall down, walls we have elaborately constructed, mostly unconsciously, that prevent us from seeing and understanding ourselves clearly. When we treat ourselves with compassion, we remember that, just like us, everyone is doing their best to learn how to live, has insecurities and fears, and has made mistakes. We no longer fall into the trap of measuring ourselves with our perception of others or with an idealized version of who we ought to be. We more accurately learn to measure ourselves with the person we used to be, noting the progress we have made, the lessons we have learned, as well as the ones we are still learning. Compassion unlocks the door for us to become more self-reflective and self-accepting and to authentically assess the attitudes, habits, and tendencies that nurture us—as well as those that don't. This allows us to take risks, make mistakes, and be okay. How else will we grow?

Today be compassionate with yourself. When you notice judgments about yourself, pride, or indignation arising, take a breath, try to let your walls fall down, and respond with compassion.

COMPASSION EXERCISE FIVE, DAY ONE **DATE:**

Morning Prayers and/or Reflection

MORNING REFLECTION

- You have a life of recovery filled with support and opportunities. Every day is a new opportunity and fresh start if you choose to take advantage of it.

- Remember that you are not the center of the universe but a valuable part of it. The events that happen in your life, whether you label them good or bad, are all opportunities to grow, learn, and make your life more meaningful.

- Bring to mind people and things you are grateful for. Make them relevant and personal.

- Take some time to reflect on the person you want to be. Set your intention to not waste this day and live it with attention and intention, cultivating the qualities that you find meaningful. Remember, the only thing that separates the person you are from the person you want to be is the action you take. Make a clear and firm commitment to your recovery today. You deserve to live a life free of addiction.

MORNING MEDITATION

Did you do it? _____   How long? _____

Set a clear intention and do your best to be compassionate with yourself. When you notice judgments about yourself, pride, or indignation arising, take a breath and look deeply. Try to let your walls down and respond with compassion.

Check in three times a day, noting what actions were skillful and unskillful regarding being honest and compassionate with yourself. Check in once in the morning (before noon), once in the afternoon (before 5:00 p.m.), and once in the evening. These should be short notes, allowing you to remember them for your evening review.

MORNING CHECK-IN

Skillful: _____

Unskillful: _____

AFTERNOON CHECK-IN

Skillful: _____

Unskillful: _____

EVENING CHECK-IN

Skillful: _____

Unskillful: _____

EVENING REVIEW

Reflecting on your day, what did you learn?

_____

_____

Were you able to be compassionate and honest with yourself? Explain.

_____

_____

What was challenging about this exercise?

_____

_____

What did you do well today?

_____

_____

How can you make amends for, or improve upon, the unskillful actions of today?

_____

_____

COMPASSION REVIEW

What were the most valuable lessons you learned this week?

_____

_____

_____

What were some of the ways you were able to use compassion to reduce suffering?

_____

_____

_____

What did you do well this week that supports your recovery?

_____

_____

_____

LOVING-KINDNESS

Loving-kindness, often described as a sincere friendliness, is the deep and sincere wish for yourself and others to be genuinely happy. It is not an attached love or kindness that is focused only on people we like or who are kind to us. In cultivating loving-kindness, we are supporting our recovery by developing the direct antidote to the mental and emotional states of anger and hatred. Essentially, it simply means that we learn to authentically wish the best for others and ourselves. Just like us, all others are trying to find their way. Just like us, they make mistakes, let people down, and engage in harmful activities. Just like us, they have the potential to change and improve.

We cannot have love and hate for the same thing at the same time. We can have love turn to hate or hate into love in a moment, but they do not exist simultaneously in the same moment. The more love and kindness we have the more difficult it is for anger and hatred to arise. As our recovery literature points out, "anger is the dubious luxury of normal people." Understanding this, we can recognize the value of consciously cultivating the immeasurable attitude of loving-kindness. As it grows within us, it limits the space available for harmful and unhealthy attitudes to take root.

Loving-Kindness Exercise One

"Love is the will to extend one's self for the purpose of nurturing one's own or another's spiritual growth."

M. SCOTT PECK

Understanding our emotions is a critical part of our recovery. If we are going to grow and flourish in our lives, we need to be able to have healthy relationships with ourselves and others and look more deeply at how we view love.

We often confuse many of the warm and/or powerful emotions we feel with love. The feelings associated with love can be a reflection of our love or, as is often the case, they can reflect our attachment to someone or something. In either case, the feelings we associate, correctly or incorrectly, with love will come and go while love itself can remain. We can love people we don't like very much; we can love people with whom we don't agree; and, of course, we can love people we do like and with whom we enjoy spending time. As Peck's quote points out, love is an intention and action that springs from a heartfelt desire for you and others to develop your highest potential and become genuinely happy.

There is a problem in the common practice of confusing attachment with love. As mentioned earlier, when others make us feel good, we can mistake our feelings for them as love. However, if we investigate, we may find that, instead of being an unconditional love that truly wants the best for the others, our feeling of love is actually contingent on how those people make us feel. When they stop doing the things that make us feel good, or start to treat us in ways we dislike, our love can turn into resentment and even hatred. People who have been friends for years can wind up not speaking to each other. A once-happy marriage can end with the couple unable to be in the same room with each other.

In such cases, what we assume to be love is really an attachment to the good feelings that arise in us when others behave in ways we like. It is this attachment, confused for love, that creates an incredible amount of suffering in our lives. When we love someone, we want them to be truly happy; we don't have an attachment to them making us feel happy. To better understand the distinction, it is helpful to recognize the action rather than the feeling of love, such as getting up in the middle of night to help another when we would really rather sleep. It might not feel good at the moment, but it is a more accurate reflection of the degree of love we have to share.

For the next two days, reflect upon the difference between attachment and love. Throughout the day, do your best to identify the acts of love around you, such as people extending themselves for another's personal growth or comfort, and engage in as many as you can.

LOVING-KINDNESS EXERCISE ONE, DAY ONE   DATE:

Morning Prayers and/or Reflection

MORNING REFLECTION

- You have a life of recovery filled with support and opportunities. Every day is a new opportunity and fresh start if you choose to take advantage of it.

- Remember that you are not the center of the universe but a valuable part of it. The events that happen in your life, whether you label them good or bad, are all opportunities to grow, learn, and make your life more meaningful.

- Bring to mind people and things you are grateful for. Make them relevant and personal.

- Take some time to reflect on the person you want to be. Set your intention to not waste this day and live it with attention and intention, cultivating the qualities that you find meaningful. Remember, the only thing that separates the person you are from the person you want to be is the action you take. Make a clear and firm commitment to your recovery today. You deserve to live a life free of addiction.

MORNING MEDITATION

Did you do it? _____   How long? _____

Set a clear intention and do your best to reflect upon the difference between attachment and love. Throughout the day, do your best to identify the acts of love—people extending themselves for another's personal growth or comfort—around you and engage in as many as you can.

Check in three times a day, noting what actions were skillful and unskillful regarding loving-kindness. Check in once in the morning (before noon), once in the afternoon (before 5:00 p.m.), and once in the evening. These should be short notes, allowing you to remember them for your evening review.

MORNING CHECK-IN

Skillful: _____

Unskillful: _____

AFTERNOON CHECK-IN

Skillful: _____

Unskillful: _____

EVENING CHECK-IN

Skillful: _____

Unskillful: _____

EVENING REVIEW

Reflecting on your day, what did you learn?

_____

_____

How was this loving-kindness activity helpful?

_____

_____

What was challenging about this activity?

_____

_____

What did you do well today?

_____

_____

How can you make amends for, or improve upon, the unskillful actions of today?

_____

_____

LOVING-KINDNESS EXERCISE ONE, DAY TWO   DATE:

Morning Prayers and/or Reflection

MORNING REFLECTION

- You have a life of recovery filled with support and opportunities. Every day is a new opportunity and fresh start if you choose to take advantage of it.

- Remember that you are not the center of the universe but a valuable part of it. The events that happen in your life, whether you label them good or bad, are all opportunities to grow, learn, and make your life more meaningful.

- Bring to mind people and things you are grateful for. Make them relevant and personal.

- Take some time to reflect on the person you want to be. Set your intention to not waste this day and live it with attention and intention, cultivating the qualities that you find meaningful. Remember, the only thing that separates the person you are from the person you want to be is the action you take. Make a clear and firm commitment to your recovery today. You deserve to live a life free of addiction.

MORNING MEDITATION

Did you do it? _____ How long? _____

Set a clear intention and do your best to reflect upon the difference between attachment and love. Throughout the day, do your best to identify the acts of love—people extending themselves for another's personal growth or comfort—around you and engage in as many as you can.

Check in three times a day, noting what actions were skillful and unskillful regarding loving-kindness. Check in once in the morning (before noon), once in the afternoon (before 5:00 p.m.), and once in the evening. These should be short notes, allowing you to remember them for your evening review.

MORNING CHECK-IN

Skillful: _____

Unskillful: _____

AFTERNOON CHECK-IN

Skillful: _____

Unskillful: _____

EVENING CHECK-IN

Skillful: _____

Unskillful: _____

EVENING REVIEW

Reflecting on your day, what did you learn?

_____

_____

How was your activity with loving-kindness helpful?

_____

_____

What was challenging about this activity?

_____

_____

What did you do well today?

_____

_____

How can you make amends for, or improve upon, the unskillful actions of today?

_____

_____

Loving-Kindness Exercise Two

> *"What does love look like? It has the hands to help others. It has
> the feet to hasten to the poor and needy. It has eyes to see misery
> and want. It has the ears to hear the sighs and sorrows of men.
> That is what love looks like."*
>
> ST. AUGUSTINE

Cultivating loving-kindness is beneficial for all of us. The more we have the better we feel and the more we can improve our lives and the lives of others. Love has only one motivation: to be truly helpful. With loving-kindness, we develop an understanding of our connection to others, our communities, the environment, and the world.

Instead of being egocentric, or the center of our own universe, and focusing only on our own needs and desires, it is valuable to recognize that we owe everything we have to the efforts of others and the resources available to us. It is our exaggerated, self-centered attitude that fueled our addiction. The more we focused on ourselves the more isolated we became from others. We forgot that our recovery, education, work, clothing, vehicles, food, recreation, and home—literally everything we have and get to do—is dependent upon others. There is no "us" without others. We are in this together and we affect each other.

If we want lasting happiness, it is essential that others be happy, healthy, and flourishing. When others are flourishing, our communities are flourishing and our lives are filled with more opportunities. When others are suffering and don't have their needs met, our communities are suffering, economically and emotionally. When others have resources and opportunities to develop their potential and dreams, they are not harming themselves or others or committing crimes.

Recognizing our shared humanity and our interdependence is the foundation of loving-kindness. Everyone has struggles, worries, and concerns just like us. As we help others, we not only improve the world, we also improve our own lives. In the process, we also add to the reservoir of loving-kindness within us, having more to draw from during difficult times.

For the next three days, be an example of what love looks like. Let the words of St. Augustine inspire you to be as helpful as you can in your actions and interactions.

LOVING-KINDNESS EXERCISE TWO, DAY ONE   DATE:

Morning Prayers and/or Reflection

MORNING REFLECTION

- You have a life of recovery filled with support and opportunities. Every day is a new opportunity and fresh start if you choose to take advantage of it.

- Remember that you are not the center of the universe but a valuable part of it. The events that happen in your life, whether you label them good or bad, are all opportunities to grow, learn, and make your life more meaningful.

- Bring to mind people and things you are grateful for. Make them relevant and personal.

- Take some time to reflect on the person you want to be. Set your intention to not waste this day and live it with attention and intention, cultivating the qualities that you find meaningful. Remember, the only thing that separates the person you are from the person you want to be is the action you take. Make a clear and firm commitment to your recovery today. You deserve to live a life free of addiction.

MORNING MEDITATION

Did you do it? _____ How long? _____

Set a clear intention and do your best to be an example of what love looks like. Try to be as helpful as you can in your actions and interactions.

Check in three times a day, noting what actions were skillful and unskillful regarding loving-kindness. Check in once in the morning (before noon), once in the afternoon (before 5:00 p.m.), and once in the evening. These should be short notes, allowing you to remember them for your evening review.

MORNING CHECK-IN

Skillful: _____

Unskillful: _____

AFTERNOON CHECK-IN

Skillful: _____

Unskillful: _____

EVENING CHECK-IN

Skillful: _____

Unskillful: _____

EVENING REVIEW

Reflecting on your day, what did you learn?

_____

_____

How was your activity with loving-kindness helpful?

_____

_____

What was challenging about this activity?

_____

_____

What did you do well today?

_____

_____

How can you make amends for, or improve upon, the unskillful actions of today?

_____

_____

LOVING-KINDNESS EXERCISE TWO, DAY TWO   DATE:

Morning Prayers and/or Reflection

MORNING REFLECTION

- You have a life of recovery filled with support and opportunities. Every day is a new opportunity and fresh start if you choose to take advantage of it.

- Remember that you are not the center of the universe but a valuable part of it. The events that happen in your life, whether you label them good or bad, are all opportunities to grow, learn, and make your life more meaningful.

- Bring to mind people and things you are grateful for. Make them relevant and personal.

- Take some time to reflect on the person you want to be. Set your intention to not waste this day and live it with attention and intention, cultivating the qualities that you find meaningful. Remember, the only thing that separates the person you are from the person you want to be is the action you take. Make a clear and firm commitment to your recovery today. You deserve to live a life free of addiction.

MORNING MEDITATION

Did you do it? _____   How long? _____

Set a clear intention and do your best to be an example of what love looks like. Try to be as helpful as you can in your actions and interactions.

Check in three times a day, noting what actions were skillful and unskillful regarding loving-kindness. Check in once in the morning (before noon), once in the afternoon (before 5:00 p.m.), and once in the evening. These should be short notes, allowing you to remember them for your evening review.

MORNING CHECK-IN

Skillful: _____

Unskillful: _____

AFTERNOON CHECK-IN

Skillful: _____

Unskillful: _____

EVENING CHECK-IN

Skillful: _____

Unskillful: _____

EVENING REVIEW

Reflecting on your day, what did you learn?

_____

_____

How was your loving-kindness exercise helpful?

_____

_____

What was challenging about this exercise?

_____

_____

What did you do well today?

_____

_____

How can you make amends for, or improve upon, the unskillful actions of today?

_____

_____

LOVING-KINDNESS EXERCISE TWO, DAY THREE   DATE:

Morning Prayers and/or Reflection

MORNING REFLECTION

- You have a life of recovery filled with support and opportunities. Every day is a new opportunity and fresh start if you choose to take advantage of it.

- Remember that you are not the center of the universe but a valuable part of it. The events that happen in your life, whether you label them good or bad, are all opportunities to grow, learn, and make your life more meaningful.

- Bring to mind people and things you are grateful for. Make them relevant and personal.

- Take some time to reflect on the person you want to be. Set your intention to not waste this day and live it with attention and intention, cultivating the qualities that you find meaningful. Remember, the only thing that separates the person you are from the person you want to be is the action you take. Make a clear and firm commitment to your recovery today. You deserve to live a life free of addiction.

MORNING MEDITATION

Did you do it? _____   How long? _____

Set a clear intention and do your best to be an example of what love looks like. Try to be as helpful as you can in your actions and interactions.

Check in three times a day, noting what actions were skillful and unskillful regarding loving-kindness. Check in once in the morning (before noon), once in the afternoon (before 5:00 p.m.), and once in the evening. These should be short notes, allowing you to remember them for your evening review.

MORNING CHECK-IN

Skillful: _____

Unskillful: _____

AFTERNOON CHECK-IN

Skillful: _____

Unskillful: _____

EVENING CHECK-IN

Skillful: _____

Unskillful: _____

EVENING REVIEW

Reflecting on your day, what did you learn?

_____

_____

How was your activity with loving-kindness helpful?

_____

_____

What was challenging about this activity?

_____

_____

What did you do well today?

_____

_____

How can you make amends for, or improve upon, the unskillful actions of today?

_____

_____

Loving-Kindness Exercise Three

"If in our daily life we can smile . . ..
This is the most basic kind of peace work."

THICH NHAT HANH

One of the easiest ways to express and share our loving-kindness with others is with a smile. Smiling also has incredible benefits for all of us. Scientists, philosophers, and spiritual teachers agree that smiling can transform us and the world around us. Research studies have shown that smiling

- feels good, has a physiological effect on us, and improves our mood;

- is contagious and lifts the moods of those around us;

- makes us appear more appealing to others;

- can make us live longer, according to a 2010 Wayne State University research project.

In recovery, we have an opportunity to cultivate joy instead of despair. Sometimes that can be accomplished with something as profoundly simple as a smile. As Thich Nhat Hanh's quote also points out, our smiles can truly benefit others by conveying our own happiness when greeting or being with them. They feel welcome, appreciated, and safe. We all know the difference we feel when we are greeted with a warm, loving smile rather than a scowl or even a look of indifference. How we attend to others has an effect on them and our interaction with them. We can even alter the tension in a room with a sincere smile that expresses our love, acceptance, and appreciation.

Today engage in the most basic kind of peace work: smiling. Do your best to make it a sincere reflection of your kindness and love. It can be helpful to recall all the kindness you have experienced in your life and reflect upon it throughout the day.

LOVING-KINDNESS EXERCISE THREE   **DATE:**

Morning Prayers and/or Reflection

MORNING REFLECTION

- You have a life of recovery filled with support and opportunities. Every day is a new opportunity and fresh start if you choose to take advantage of it.

- Remember that you are not the center of the universe but a valuable part of it. The events that happen in your life, whether you label them good or bad, are all opportunities to grow, learn, and make your life more meaningful.

- Bring to mind people and things you are grateful for. Make them relevant and personal.

- Take some time to reflect on the person you want to be. Set your intention to not waste this day and live it with attention and intention, cultivating the qualities that you find meaningful. Remember, the only thing that separates the person you are from the person you want to be is the action you take. Make a clear and firm commitment to your recovery today. You deserve to live a life free of addiction.

MORNING MEDITATION

Did you do it? _____   How long? _____

Set a clear intention and do your best to engage in the most basic kind of peace work: smiling. Do your best to greet others with a heartfelt smile. Notice how that affects your interactions.

Check in three times a day, noting what actions were skillful and unskillful regarding smiling. Check in once in the morning (before noon), once in the afternoon (before 5:00 p.m.), and once in the evening. These should be short notes, allowing you to remember them for your evening review.

MORNING CHECK-IN

Skillful: _____

Unskillful: _____

AFTERNOON CHECK-IN

Skillful: _____

Unskillful: _____

EVENING CHECK-IN

Skillful: _____

Unskillful: _____

EVENING REVIEW

Reflecting on your day, what did you learn?

_____

_____

How was smiling helpful?

_____

_____

What was challenging about this activity?

_____

_____

What did you do well today?

_____

_____

How can you make amends for, or improve upon, the unskillful actions of today?

_____

_____

Loving-Kindness Exercise Four

*"A hundred times every day I remind myself that my inner
and outer life depend on the labors of others."*

ALBERT EINSTEIN

Remembering the kindness of others helps us develop loving-kindness. How many people have helped us find and live in recovery? When we reflect upon the many times friends or family have helped us in difficult times—offering emotional support, guidance, a helping hand, a shoulder to lean on, financial aid, or inspiration—we naturally have a feeling, a gratitude and a desire, to help them in any way we can.

We have been helped so many times there is no way to remember them all! Just trying to recall all the people we are aware of who have helped us would be impossible. Einstein's quote reminds us that, in addition to all those we know about, countless others, through their efforts and struggles, have also contributed to the life we have today. As mentioned previously, it is helpful to remember that everything we have is the result of the efforts of others, most of whom we will never know.

Just as reflecting on the kindness of our friends and family members helps us develop gratitude and loving-kindness toward them, reflecting on the efforts of those we don't know—those who paved the roads we drive on, harvested the food we eat, made the clothes we wear, educated us or our children, worked to keep our communities safe and clean, and provided mental and physical health care—can also provide us with a deep sense of gratitude and an eagerness to return their kindness.

Take a little time today to reflect upon all the help you have received in your life. As you engage in your day, see if you can recognize how the efforts of others contribute to the life you get to live and attempt to return the favor, even in some small way.

LOVING-KINDNESS EXERCISE FOUR   DATE:

Morning Prayers and/or Reflection

MORNING REFLECTION

- You have a life of recovery filled with support and opportunities. Every day is a new opportunity and fresh start if you choose to take advantage of it.

- Remember that you are not the center of the universe but a valuable part of it. The events that happen in your life, whether you label them good or bad, are all opportunities to grow, learn, and make your life more meaningful.

- Bring to mind people and things you are grateful for. Make them relevant and personal.

- Take some time to reflect on the person you want to be. Set your intention to not waste this day and live it with attention and intention, cultivating the qualities that you find meaningful. Remember, the only thing that separates the person you are from the person you want to be is the action you take. Make a clear and firm commitment to your recovery today. You deserve to live a life free of addiction.

MORNING MEDITATION

Did you do it? _____   How long? _____

Take a little time to reflect upon all the help you have received in your life. Set a clear intention to do your best to recognize how the efforts of others contribute to the life you get to live and see if you can return the favor, even in some small way.

Check in three times a day, noting what actions were skillful and unskillful regarding today's exercise. Check in once in the morning (before noon), once in the afternoon (before 5:00 p.m.), and once in the evening. These should be short notes, allowing you to remember them for your evening review.

MORNING CHECK-IN

Skillful: _____

Unskillful: _____

AFTERNOON CHECK-IN

Skillful: _____

Unskillful: _____

EVENING CHECK-IN

Skillful: _____

Unskillful: _____

EVENING REVIEW

Reflecting on your day, what did you learn?

_____

_____

How was today's exercise helpful?

_____

_____

What was challenging about this exercise?

_____

_____

What did you do well today?

_____

_____

How can you make amends for, or improve upon, the unskillful actions of today?

_____

_____

Loving-Kindness Exercise Five

"It is very important to generate a good attitude, a good heart,
as much as possible. From this, happiness in both the short term
and the long term for both yourself and others will come."

14TH DALAI LAMA

Though there are many studies clearly demonstrating that people with a positive attitude and an open and kind heart are happier, healthier, and tend to live longer, we probably knew this to be true before the research. We also know that anger, stress, worry, and fear, or a negative attitude, obviously do not support recovery or create happiness for ourselves or others. We feel better and are more able to engage in our lives when we are optimistic and openhearted. This carries over into our interactions with others and improves those interactions.

As true as this is, a positive attitude is often misinterpreted to mean that everything in our lives is just fine, we have no problems, or we should just think happy thoughts. Just thinking happy thoughts does not solve real-life problems. Life is messy, and we have to deal with things—everyone does. A good attitude does not mean we ignore challenges and difficulties; it means we can develop the confidence to meet them as best we can, knowing that doing our best in any situation is what matters most.

Loving-kindness is a valuable tool that helps us face life's challenges more skillfully, especially with others. Seeing ourselves connected with others, recognizing their value and their struggles, and developing loving-kindness toward them makes it more difficult for harmful attitudes—such as jealousy, resentment, bitterness, and anger—to arise. In this way, loving-kindness supports healthy, mental states and attitudes that help us become problem solvers instead of problem dwellers. You may find that adopting a we-centered attitude instead of a me-centered attitude solves many problems on its own.

Today do your best to initiate and maintain a good, healthy, and realistic problem-solving attitude.

LOVING-KINDNESS EXERCISE FIVE   **DATE:**

Morning Prayers and/or Reflection

MORNING REFLECTION

- You have a life of recovery filled with support and opportunities. Every day is a new opportunity and fresh start if you choose to take advantage of it.

- Remember that you are not the center of the universe but a valuable part of it. The events that happen in your life, whether you label them good or bad, are all opportunities to grow, learn, and make your life more meaningful.

- Bring to mind people and things you are grateful for. Make them relevant and personal.

- Take some time to reflect on the person you want to be. Set your intention to not waste this day and live it with attention and intention, cultivating the qualities that you find meaningful. Remember, the only thing that separates the person you are from the person you want to be is the action you take. Make a clear and firm commitment to your recovery today. You deserve to live a life free of addiction.

MORNING MEDITATION

Did you do it? _____   How long? _____

    Set a clear intention to do your best to initiate and maintain a good, healthy, realistic, problem-solving attitude.

    Check in three times a day, noting what actions were skillful and unskillful regarding today's exercise. Check in once in the morning (before noon), once in the afternoon (before 5:00 p.m.), and once in the evening. These should be short notes, allowing you to remember them for your evening review.

MORNING CHECK-IN

Skillful: _____

Unskillful: _____

AFTERNOON CHECK-IN

Skillful: _____

Unskillful: _____

EVENING CHECK-IN

Skillful: _____

Unskillful: _____

EVENING REVIEW

Reflecting on your day, what did you learn?

_____

_____

How was today's exercise helpful?

_____

_____

What was challenging about this exercise?

_____

_____

What did you do well today?

_____

_____

How can you make amends for, or improve upon, the unskillful actions of today?

_____

_____

LOVING-KINDNESS REVIEW

What were the most valuable lessons you learned this week?

_____

_____

_____

What were some of the ways loving-kindness was beneficial for you?

_____

_____

_____

What did you do well this week that supports your recovery?

_____

_____

_____

ACTION

There is an old piece of wisdom that says you cannot think yourself into right living, but you can live yourself into right thinking. How many times have we set good intentions and not been able to follow through? Alternatively, how many great epiphanies have we had that we decided to integrate into our lives, only to see them fall away?

Living mindfully in recovery, we learn to live with attention and intention, guided by our values. We develop the ability to consciously bring awareness into our daily activities. As we do this, we also become aware of how our addiction habits, tendencies, and beliefs prevent us from living in alignment with our values. This is the beginning of wisdom and true recovery, identifying within ourselves that which prevents us from being who we really want to be.

What are the habits, tendencies, and misperceptions, in the guise of finding pleasure and acceptance, that bring about suffering and isolation? The only way to remove these is to recognize and understand them. To recognize and understand them, we need to be conscious of how they arise and prevent us from living the life we find valuable and meaningful.

In the following exercises, you will practice intentional living through transformative action and see if you can discover some of the habits and tendencies that support as well as the ones that hinder you.

Action Exercise One

"But we are first of all called to a more immediate
and exalted task: that of creating our own lives."

THOMAS MERTON

We have all spent time in deep and meaningful discussions about difficulties in the world and possible solutions to them. We have also spent time on the same topics without much depth or reflection. Our discussions about problems in the world, communities, schools, the price of gas, what is fair and not fair, the cost of living, or health care can come up frequently and spontaneously. We may even have a few ideas about how our local government or market could run more effectively.

With all this external focus, we often forget to have the deeper reflections and conversations about improving the depth and quality of our own lives. In general, most people wake up and engage in their days without taking a little time to reflect upon the meaning and purpose of their lives. Our days can be filled with activities, things to do, and wide-ranging discussions. We may have duties to fulfill, obligations to be honored, or fun-filled adventures to be discovered. We often engage in our day without the conscious awareness of how our actions align with our inner desires to live truly meaningful lives.

As Merton's quote points out, our most immediate and exalted task is to develop our own highest potential and create purposeful lives. As we cultivate our lives in recovery, we can develop inner strength, resiliency, and integrity. In doing so, we will be in a much better position to benefit our families, friends, and the world. It is important to remember that as we improve so does the world. Therefore, while it is of critical importance to have deep and meaningful conversations about the problems that confront our communities and possible solutions, it is even more important to engage in discussions, reflections, and actions that help improve our own lives. In that way, we will have much more to offer our communities.

For the next two days, reflect upon and clearly identify a habit or attitude that you would like to develop to improve your life. Set your intention to cultivate it, not just today, but from now on.

ACTION EXERCISE ONE, DAY ONE   DATE:

Morning Prayers and/or Reflection

MORNING REFLECTION

- You have a life of recovery filled with support and opportunities. Every day is a new opportunity and fresh start if you choose to take advantage of it.

- Remember that you are not the center of the universe but a valuable part of it. The events that happen in your life, whether you label them good or bad, are all opportunities to grow, learn, and make your life more meaningful.

- Bring to mind people and things you are grateful for. Make them relevant and personal.

- Take some time to reflect on the person you want to be. Set your intention to not waste this day and live it with attention and intention, cultivating the qualities that you find meaningful. Remember, the only thing that separates the person you are from the person you want to be is the action you take. Make a clear and firm commitment to your recovery today. You deserve to live a life free of addiction.

MORNING MEDITATION

Did you do it? _____   How long? _____

Set an intention to reflect upon and clearly identify a habit or attitude that you would like to develop to improve your life. Set your intention to cultivate it, not just today, but from now on.

Check in three times a day, noting what actions were skillful and unskillful regarding your habit/attitude. Check in once in the morning (before noon), once in the afternoon (before 5:00 p.m.), and once in the evening. These should be short notes, allowing you to remember them for your evening review.

MORNING CHECK-IN

Skillful: _____

Unskillful: _____

AFTERNOON CHECK-IN

Skillful: _____

Unskillful: _____

EVENING CHECK-IN

Skillful: _____

Unskillful: _____

EVENING REVIEW

Reflecting on your day, what did you learn?

_____

_____

How was today's exercise helpful?

_____

_____

What was challenging about this exercise?

_____

_____

What did you do well today?

_____

_____

How can you make amends for, or improve upon, the unskillful actions of today?

_____

_____

ACTION EXERCISE ONE, DAY TWO   **DATE:**

Morning Prayers and/or Reflection

MORNING REFLECTION

- You have a life of recovery filled with support and opportunities. Every day is a new opportunity and fresh start if you choose to take advantage of it.

- Remember that you are not the center of the universe but a valuable part of it. The events that happen in your life, whether you label them good or bad, are all opportunities to grow, learn, and make your life more meaningful.

- Bring to mind people and things you are grateful for. Make them relevant and personal.

- Take some time to reflect on the person you want to be. Set your intention to not waste this day and live it with attention and intention, cultivating the qualities that you find meaningful. Remember, the only thing that separates the person you are from the person you want to be is the action you take. Make a clear and firm commitment to your recovery today. You deserve to live a life free of addiction.

MORNING MEDITATION

Did you do it? _____   How long? _____

Set an intention to reflect upon and clearly identify a habit or attitude that you would like to develop to improve your life. Set your intention to cultivate it, not just today, but from now on.

Check in three times a day, noting what actions were skillful and unskillful regarding your habit/attitude. Check in once in the morning (before noon), once in the afternoon (before 5:00 p.m.), and once in the evening. These should be short notes, allowing you to remember them for your evening review.

MORNING CHECK-IN

Skillful: _____

Unskillful: _____

AFTERNOON CHECK-IN

Skillful: _____

Unskillful: _____

EVENING CHECK-IN

Skillful: _____

Unskillful: _____

EVENING REVIEW

Reflecting on your day, what did you learn?

_____

_____

How was today's exercise helpful?

_____

_____

What was challenging about this exercise?

_____

_____

What did you do well today?

_____

_____

How can you make amends for, or improve upon, the unskillful actions of today?

_____

_____

Action Exercise Two

*"A little knowledge that acts is worth infinitely
more than much knowledge that is idle."*

KAHLIL GIBRAN

How many times have we learned the same lesson again and again? How many times have we known better but went ahead and made a poor choice anyway? How much valuable wisdom has been passed on to us that we do not act upon? Our road to recovery is filled with poor choices that went against our own wisdom.

It is often said that we already have our own answers. There is even a book about it, *All I Really Need to Know I Learned in Kindergarten*. While the title may not be entirely true, there is a great deal of wisdom and truth in the lessons we have learned since childhood. Unfortunately, there is a tendency to dismiss such invaluable wisdom as childish without recognizing its true value. Whether we are studying classic philosophers such as Aristotle, ancient spiritual texts, or our recovery literature, we will find many of the same lessons we learned in childhood. Our elders have been sharing their wisdom with us throughout our lives.

More often than we realize, our problem is not that we do not know what to do to improve our lives; it is that we don't put into action the lessons we have already learned. Many of them are extremely simple and straightforward: if we want to feel worthy and valuable, we do worthy and valuable things; if we want to develop patience, kindness, acceptance, and love, we practice patience, kindness, acceptance, and love; if we want to develop inner peace, well-being, and resiliency, we engage in activities with integrity that are in alignment with our values; if we want good friends, we become a good friend. Life is rarely as complicated as we make it. It is usually simply lacking one ingredient that will improve it: action.

For the next two days, take some good advice, even if it is your own, and put it into action. Reflect upon some advice you have given others or have received that you felt was truly helpful, then put it into action.

ACTION EXERCISE TWO, DAY ONE   DATE:

Morning Prayers and/or Reflection

MORNING REFLECTION

- You have a life of recovery filled with support and opportunities. Every day is a new opportunity and fresh start if you choose to take advantage of it.

- Remember that you are not the center of the universe but a valuable part of it. The events that happen in your life, whether you label them good or bad, are all opportunities to grow, learn, and make your life more meaningful.

- Bring to mind people and things you are grateful for. Make them relevant and personal.

- Take some time to reflect on the person you want to be. Set your intention to not waste this day and live it with attention and intention, cultivating the qualities that you find meaningful. Remember, the only thing that separates the person you are from the person you want to be is the action you take. Make a clear and firm commitment to your recovery today. You deserve to live a life free of addiction.

MORNING MEDITATION

Did you do it? _____   How long? _____

Set a clear intention to take some good advice, even if it is your own, and put it into action. Reflect upon some advice that you have given others or you have received that you felt was truly helpful. Then put that advice into action.

Check in three times a day, noting what actions were skillful and unskillful regarding the lessons you want to put into action. Check in once in the morning (before noon), once in the afternoon (before 5:00 p.m.), and once in the evening. These should be short notes, allowing you to remember them for your evening review.

MORNING CHECK-IN

Skillful: _____

Unskillful: _____

AFTERNOON CHECK-IN

Skillful: _____

Unskillful: _____

EVENING CHECK-IN

Skillful: _____

Unskillful: _____

EVENING REVIEW

Reflecting on your day, what did you learn?

_____

_____

How was today's exercise helpful?

_____

_____

What was challenging about this exercise?

_____

_____

What did you do well today?

_____

_____

How can you make amends for, or improve upon, the unskillful actions of today?

_____

_____

ACTION EXERCISE TWO, DAY TWO　　　　　DATE:

Morning Prayers and/or Reflection

MORNING REFLECTION

- You have a life of recovery filled with support and opportunities. Every day is a new opportunity and fresh start if you choose to take advantage of it.

- Remember that you are not the center of the universe but a valuable part of it. The events that happen in your life, whether you label them good or bad, are all opportunities to grow, learn, and make your life more meaningful.

- Bring to mind people and things you are grateful for. Make them relevant and personal.

- Take some time to reflect on the person you want to be. Set your intention to not waste this day and live it with attention and intention, cultivating the qualities that you find meaningful. Remember, the only thing that separates the person you are from the person you want to be is the action you take. Make a clear and firm commitment to your recovery today. You deserve to live a life free of addiction.

MORNING MEDITATION

Did you do it? _____　How long? _____

Set a clear intention to take some good advice, even if it is your own, and put it into action. Reflect upon some advice that you have given others or you have received that you felt was truly helpful. Then put that advice into action.

Check in three times a day, noting what actions were skillful and unskillful regarding the lessons you want to put into action. Check in once in the morning (before noon), once in the afternoon (before 5:00 p.m.), and once in the evening. These should be short notes, allowing you to remember them for your evening review.

MORNING CHECK-IN

Skillful: _____

Unskillful: _____

AFTERNOON CHECK-IN

Skillful: _____

Unskillful: _____

EVENING CHECK-IN

Skillful: _____

Unskillful: _____

EVENING REVIEW

Reflecting on your day, what did you learn?

_____

_____

How was today's exercise helpful?

_____

_____

What was challenging about this exercise?

_____

_____

What did you do well today?

_____

_____

How can you make amends for, or improve upon, the unskillful actions of today?

_____

_____

Action Exercise Three

"When we do the best that we can, we never know
what miracle is wrought in our life."

HELEN KELLER

Throughout all the ups and downs of recovery, there is one thing we can count on: we will never regret doing our best. Of course, we can also be sure that in our recovery there will be challenges, opportunities, and complete unknowns. Even doing our best, we will make mistakes.

Though we can make plans, do our diligent research, and plot our future, we really don't know how it will all turn out and who we will meet along the way. We all know what it is like to have things turn out in unexpected ways. So many things in our lives have turned out in ways we never could have imagined years ago. Over our lifetimes, old friends will go and new friends will come, many will help us and we will help many. We will have difficulties and encounter challenging people in ways we had never expected and we will have opportunities we never imagined greet us when we least expect it. Throughout it all, though we may have regrets, we will never regret doing our best.

When we try to do our best, we have an opportunity not only to improve the quality of our lives but also to improve the world. Our actions have ripples beyond our ability to measure. When you simply try to do the minimum, giving as little attention or effort as possible to your actions and interactions, how do you feel about yourself and your actions? On the other hand, what does it feel like when you pick up the phone to reach out to a friend just when they needed to hear your voice? How might it change your day and a stranger's day if you help him or her in some way? How might a little extra effort at work help your co-workers, clients, or customers in ways you may never imagine? As we travel, a little politeness and kindness go a long way and set the tone for all those traveling with us. A little extra attention in our interactions improves them and provides opportunities that may otherwise slip by. At the end of the day, we always support our recovery and sleep a little better when we know we tried to do our best.

For the next two days, try to do your best at whatever activities you engage in. Remember that doing your best does not mean being the best. This is not a competition. The point is not to be better than others but to work on being a better version of yourself, embodying the values you find meaningful.

ACTION EXERCISE THREE, DAY ONE   **DATE:**

Morning Prayers and/or Reflection

MORNING REFLECTION

- You have a life of recovery filled with support and opportunities. Every day is a new opportunity and fresh start if you choose to take advantage of it.

- Remember that you are not the center of the universe but a valuable part of it. The events that happen in your life, whether you label them good or bad, are all opportunities to grow, learn, and make your life more meaningful.

- Bring to mind people and things you are grateful for. Make them relevant and personal.

- Take some time to reflect on the person you want to be. Set your intention to not waste this day and live it with attention and intention, cultivating the qualities that you find meaningful. Remember, the only thing that separates the person you are from the person you want to be is the action you take. Make a clear and firm commitment to your recovery today. You deserve to live a life free of addiction.

MORNING MEDITATION

Did you do it? _____   How long? _____

Set a clear intention to try to do your best at whatever activities you engage in. Remember that doing your best does not mean being the best: this is not a competition. The point is not to be better than others but to work on being a better version of yourself, embodying the values you find meaningful.

Check in three times a day, noting what actions were skillful and unskillful regarding doing your best. Check in once in the morning (before noon), once in the afternoon (before 5:00 p.m.), and once in the evening. These should be short notes, allowing you to remember them for your evening review.

MORNING CHECK-IN

Skillful: _____

Unskillful: _____

AFTERNOON CHECK-IN

Skillful: _____

Unskillful: _____

EVENING CHECK-IN

Skillful: _____

Unskillful: _____

EVENING REVIEW

Reflecting on your day, what did you learn?

_____

_____

How was trying to do your best today beneficial?

_____

_____

What was challenging about this exercise?

_____

_____

What did you do well today?

_____

_____

How can you make amends for, or improve upon, the unskillful actions of today?

_____

_____

ACTION EXERCISE THREE, DAY TWO   DATE:

Morning Prayers and/or Reflection

MORNING REFLECTION

- You have a life of recovery filled with support and opportunities. Every day is a new opportunity and fresh start if you choose to take advantage of it.

- Remember that you are not the center of the universe but a valuable part of it. The events that happen in your life, whether you label them good or bad, are all opportunities to grow, learn, and make your life more meaningful.

- Bring to mind people and things you are grateful for. Make them relevant and personal.

- Take some time to reflect on the person you want to be. Set your intention to not waste this day and live it with attention and intention, cultivating the qualities that you find meaningful. Remember, the only thing that separates the person you are from the person you want to be is the action you take. Make a clear and firm commitment to your recovery today. You deserve to live a life free of addiction.

MORNING MEDITATION

Did you do it? _____   How long? _____

Set a clear intention to try to do your best at whatever activities you engage in. Remember that doing your best does not mean being the best: this is not a competition. The point is not to be better than others but to work on being a better version of yourself, embodying the values you find meaningful.

Check in three times a day, noting what actions were skillful and unskillful regarding doing your best. Check in once in the morning (before noon), once in the afternoon (before 5:00 p.m.), and once in the evening. These should be short notes, allowing you to remember them for your evening review.

MORNING CHECK-IN

Skillful: _____

Unskillful: _____

AFTERNOON CHECK-IN

Skillful: _____

Unskillful: _____

EVENING CHECK-IN

Skillful: _____

Unskillful: _____

EVENING REVIEW

Reflecting on your day, what did you learn?

_____

_____

How was trying to do your best today beneficial?

_____

_____

What was challenging about this exercise?

_____

_____

What did you do well today?

_____

_____

How can you make amends for, or improve upon, the unskillful actions of today?

_____

_____

Action Exercise Four

*"Let everything you do be done as if
it makes a difference. It does."*

WILLIAM JAMES

We will never truly know how much our thoughts and actions affect us and others. Even the subtlest interactions leave an imprint on us and them. A slight smile may release stress and worry in another person. An unconscious scowl resulting from our inner struggles can create insecurity and resentment in someone else. Helping another find recovery affects the lives of many people we will never know, in ways we cannot begin to imagine. Picking up a piece of trash as we walk down the street might make us feel better and inspire others without our knowing. The extra clothes we donate to charity may give others warmth in the winter, and money or resources given to any charity provide for countless others. Where we work, how we spend our money, where we shop, and how we treat our family, friends, and neighbors all have ripple effects beyond our awareness.

The thoughts and attitudes we recall again and again become more deeply rooted in our minds. Just as walking again and again in the forest creates a path, the thoughts we think again and again create pathways in our mind. Unfortunately, many of our thoughts and attitudes are not conscious. They arise on their own, without us bringing them to mind, and can reinforce habits and tendencies that can keep us from finding real joy in recovery.

The more conscious awareness we can bring into our attitudes, thoughts, actions, and interactions with others the more opportunity we have to influence their effect on us and others. Instead of allowing our minds to be dominated by insecurity, fears, anger, or resentments, we can consciously create healthier attitudes that support recovery, resiliency, wisdom, and inspiration. The activities we engage in consciously can allow us to develop ourselves while we support our local communities and the world.

If we can bring conscious attention to our interactions with others, we can bring care and concern to them, allowing others to feel valuable and improving our relationships with those we encounter. Everything we do leaves an imprint on us and others, whether we are conscious of it or not. Living mindfully, we can develop the skills to bring attention and intention to all we think, say, and do. We can also train our thoughts and actions to support our recovery and become aware of those who undermine it.

For the next two days, bring as much attention and intention as you can to your thoughts, actions, and interactions, noting whether they support your recovery.

ACTION EXERCISE FOUR, DAY ONE   DATE:

Morning Prayers and/or Reflection

MORNING REFLECTION

- You have a life of recovery filled with support and opportunities. Every day is a new opportunity and fresh start if you choose to take advantage of it.

- Remember that you are not the center of the universe but a valuable part of it. The events that happen in your life, whether you label them good or bad, are all opportunities to grow, learn, and make your life more meaningful.

- Bring to mind people and things you are grateful for. Make them relevant and personal.

- Take some time to reflect on the person you want to be. Set your intention to not waste this day and live it with attention and intention, cultivating the qualities that you find meaningful. Remember, the only thing that separates the person you are from the person you want to be is the action you take. Make a clear and firm commitment to your recovery today. You deserve to live a life free of addiction.

MORNING MEDITATION

Did you do it? _____ How long? _____

Set a clear intention to try to bring as much attention and intention as you can to your thoughts, actions, and interactions, noting whether they support your recovery or not.

Check in three times a day, noting what was skillful and unskillful regarding actions that support your recovery. Check in once in the morning (before noon), once in the afternoon (before 5:00 p.m.), and once in the evening. These should be short notes, allowing you to remember them for your evening review.

MORNING CHECK-IN

Skillful: _____

Unskillful: _____

AFTERNOON CHECK-IN

Skillful: _____

Unskillful: _____

EVENING CHECK-IN

Skillful: _____

Unskillful: _____

EVENING REVIEW

Reflecting on your day, what did you learn?

_____

_____

What were the most valuable actions/thoughts that supported your recovery today?

_____

_____

What were the actions/thoughts that did not support your recovery?

_____

_____

What did you do well today?

_____

_____

How can you make amends for, or improve upon, the unskillful actions of today?

_____

_____

ACTION EXERCISE FOUR, DAY TWO   DATE:

Morning Prayers and/or Reflection

MORNING REFLECTION

- You have a life of recovery filled with support and opportunities. Every day is a new opportunity and fresh start if you choose to take advantage of it.

- Remember that you are not the center of the universe but a valuable part of it. The events that happen in your life, whether you label them good or bad, are all opportunities to grow, learn, and make your life more meaningful.

- Bring to mind people and things you are grateful for. Make them relevant and personal.

- Take some time to reflect on the person you want to be. Set your intention to not waste this day and live it with attention and intention, cultivating the qualities that you find meaningful. Remember, the only thing that separates the person you are from the person you want to be is the action you take. Make a clear and firm commitment to your recovery today. You deserve to live a life free of addiction.

MORNING MEDITATION

Did you do it? _____   How long? _____

Set a clear intention to try to bring as much attention and intention as you can to your thoughts, actions, and interactions, noting whether they support your recovery or not.

Check in three times a day, noting what was skillful and unskillful regarding actions that support your recovery. Check in once in the morning (before noon), once in the afternoon (before 5:00 p.m.), and once in the evening. These should be short notes, allowing you to remember them for your evening review.

MORNING CHECK-IN

Skillful: _____

Unskillful: _____

AFTERNOON CHECK-IN

Skillful: _____

Unskillful: _____

EVENING CHECK-IN

Skillful: _____

Unskillful: _____

EVENING REVIEW

Reflecting on your day, what did you learn?

_____

_____

What were the most valuable actions/thoughts that supported your recovery today?

_____

_____

What were the actions/thoughts that did not support your recovery?

_____

_____

What did you do well today?

_____

_____

How can you make amends for, or improve upon, the unskillful actions of today?

_____

_____

ACTION REVIEW

What were the most valuable lessons you learned this week?

_____

_____

_____

What were some of ways taking action was beneficial for you?

_____

_____

_____

What did you do well this week that supports your recovery?

_____

_____

_____

MORE WISDOM

This week explore the habits, tendencies, and attitudes you have developed and how they shape your experience of the world and interactions with others. This will help provide some insight into recognizing and nurturing the healthy and wise choices you make that support your recovery as well as acknowledging and letting go of the unhealthy choices. Ultimately, the goal is to gain wisdom, not simply to acquire knowledge. With wisdom in our recovery, we are able to apply the lessons we have learned in life in productive and meaningful ways.

Wisdom Exercise Two

"We all have the potential to be better than we are."

14TH DALAI LAMA

The quote by the 14th Dalai Lama contains an empowering truth we often forget: no matter how much or how little growth and meaning we feel we have achieved in our lives, we can always improve. Every day in recovery, we have the precious opportunity to improve ourselves and the quality of our lives. The key is bringing our attention back to the qualities we want to develop in ourselves and cultivating the intention to engage in activities that support our recovery and the growth we find meaningful.

As we live mindfully in recovery, bringing attention and intention into our lives, we usually discover that the person most responsible for holding us back is staring back at us from the mirror. We all have old stories and limiting beliefs about ourselves that prevent us from developing new attitudes and exploring our full potential. However, everything is changing all the time, including us. This is one of the fundamental truths of life. Despite this, we often cling to beliefs about ourselves that may no longer be true. Even simple thoughts—"I am not a morning person"; "I am not a good speaker"; "I am not good with people"; "I am not a good meditator"; "I am not patient"—are all changeable.

We do change and, more importantly, we can change consciously. We do not have to be a prisoner of old habits and beliefs that prevent us from growing in healthy and meaningful ways. As we have been learning through our experiences and reflections, it is as simple—and as difficult—as learning to keep in mind the values and qualities we find meaningful, then consciously making an effort to engage in activities that support those values and qualities. Instead of trying to think ourselves into becoming the person we want to be, we start living the life of the person we want to become. In doing so, we nurture and support the habits and tendencies that allow us to realize our full potential and, before we know it, we are growing in ways we had never imagined.

For the next two days, reinvigorate your practice. Take a little time to reflect upon a belief you have about yourself that you find limiting. Challenge it to see if, in fact, it is still true. What can you do to improve? Today make the intention to improve in a way you find meaningful.

WISDOM EXERCISE TWO, DAY ONE   **DATE:**

Morning Prayers and/or Reflection

MORNING REFLECTION

- You have a life of recovery filled with support and opportunities. Every day is a new opportunity and fresh start if you choose to take advantage of it.

- Remember that you are not the center of the universe but a valuable part of it. The events that happen in your life, whether you label them good or bad, are all opportunities to grow, learn, and make your life more meaningful.

- Bring to mind people and things you are grateful for. Make them relevant and personal.

- Take some time to reflect on the person you want to be. Set your intention to not waste this day and live it with attention and intention, cultivating the qualities that you find meaningful. Remember, the only thing that separates the person you are from the person you want to be is the action you take. Make a clear and firm commitment to your recovery today. You deserve to live a life free of addiction.

MORNING MEDITATION

Did you do it? _____   How long? _____

Write down the belief you want to challenge or quality you would like to improve. Then do your best to bear it in mind today, so you can either challenge the belief or support the quality you have chosen.

_____

_____

Check in three times a day, noting what actions were skillful and unskillful regarding your intention. Check in once in the morning (before noon), once in the afternoon (before 5:00 p.m.), and once in the evening. These should be short notes, allowing you to remember them for your evening review.

MORNING CHECK-IN

Skillful: _____

Unskillful: _____

AFTERNOON CHECK-IN

Skillful: _____

Unskillful: _____

EVENING CHECK-IN

Skillful: _____

Unskillful: _____

EVENING REVIEW

Reflecting on your day, what did you learn?

_____

_____

What were the most valuable actions/thoughts that helped you with this activity?

_____

_____

What was difficult about challenging your belief or improving yourself?

_____

_____

What did you do well today?

_____

_____

How can you make amends for, or improve upon, the unskillful actions of today?

_____

_____

WISDOM EXERCISE TWO, DAY TWO   DATE:

Morning Prayers and/or Reflection

MORNING REFLECTION

- You have a life of recovery filled with support and opportunities. Every day is a new opportunity and fresh start if you choose to take advantage of it.

- Remember that you are not the center of the universe but a valuable part of it. The events that happen in your life, whether you label them good or bad, are all opportunities to grow, learn, and make your life more meaningful.

- Bring to mind people and things you are grateful for. Make them relevant and personal.

- Take some time to reflect on the person you want to be. Set your intention to not waste this day and live it with attention and intention, cultivating the qualities that you find meaningful. Remember, the only thing that separates the person you are from the person you want to be is the action you take. Make a clear and firm commitment to your recovery today. You deserve to live a life free of addiction.

MORNING MEDITATION

Did you do it? _____   How long? _____

Write down the belief you want to challenge of quality you would like to improve. Then do your best to bear it in mind today, so you can either challenge the belief or support the quality you have chosen.

_____

_____

Check in three times a day, noting what actions were skillful and unskillful regarding your intention. Check in once in the morning (before noon), once in the afternoon (before 5:00 p.m.), and once in the evening. These should be short notes, allowing you to remember them for your evening review.

MORNING CHECK-IN

Skillful: _____

Unskillful: _____

AFTERNOON CHECK-IN

Skillful: _____

Unskillful: _____

EVENING CHECK-IN

Skillful: _____

Unskillful: _____

EVENING REVIEW

Reflecting on your day, what did you learn?

_____

_____

What were the most valuable actions/thoughts that helped you with this activity?

_____

_____

What was difficult about challenging your belief or improving yourself?

_____

_____

What did you do well today?

_____

_____

How can you make amends for, or improve upon, the unskillful actions of today?

_____

_____

Wisdom Exercise Three

"We awaken in others the same attitude
of mind that we hold toward them."

ELBERT HUBBARD

All of us in recovery know all too well that our expectations often become self-fulfilling prophecies. Though things do not always turn out the way we imagined, our preconceptions about any given activity or person have an effect. In general, people and events tend to live up to our expectations of them. We tend to see what we expect to see, which limits our view, the potential of the people we encounter, and the activities we engage in. This is especially true of people.

It is natural and a common tendency to evaluate the people we meet. Once we get to know them, we start identifying their traits and labeling them: smart, funny, interesting, know-it-all, boring, creative, mean, selfish, generous, or even dumb. These are just a few of the many labels we attach to the people in our lives.

Unfortunately, once we have labeled someone, the label tends to stick and we are rarely open to relabeling them. It is important to remember that all of us have had such labels attached to us.

At some moment in time, a label may have been true. However, no label, whether applied to us or others, can capture the entire essence of a person. When we label others, it affects us as well. It can be difficult to allow ourselves to learn or receive help from someone if we once gave them a negative label.

Hubbard's quote reminds us to be aware of our attitude and the labels we project on others. Labels affect the way we experience people. Becoming aware that we are labeling, or have a particular biased view, allows for healthier interactions and new potential in those interactions.

Each person we encounter, having had many experiences different from ours, knows more than we do about many things. If we can remember this fundamental truth, those people become teachers and we become available to learn and grow. If we recognized the value in others and treated them as valuable, how do you think our interactions would be different? We all know when people have believed in us, we have discovered our own inner resources. How could we have found recovery if people had not looked past our labels? Likewise, when we treat others with respect and dignity, we might find that they are more able to rise to their full potential.

For the next two days, be aware of how your labels and attitudes toward others affect your interactions with them. See if you can engage others with an attitude of respect and dignity that includes a vision of their potential.

WISDOM EXERCISE THREE, DAY ONE   DATE:

Morning Prayers and/or Reflection

MORNING REFLECTION

- You have a life of recovery filled with support and opportunities. Every day is a new opportunity and fresh start if you choose to take advantage of it.

- Remember that you are not the center of the universe but a valuable part of it. The events that happen in your life, whether you label them good or bad, are all opportunities to grow, learn, and make your life more meaningful.

- Bring to mind people and things you are grateful for. Make them relevant and personal.

- Take some time to reflect on the person you want to be. Set your intention to not waste this day and live it with attention and intention, cultivating the qualities that you find meaningful. Remember, the only thing that separates the person you are from the person you want to be is the action you take. Make a clear and firm commitment to your recovery today. You deserve to live a life free of addiction.

MORNING MEDITATION

Did you do it? _____   How long? _____

Set a clear intention to be aware of how your labels and attitudes toward others affect your interactions with them. See if you can engage with others with an attitude of respect and dignity that includes a vision of their potential.

Check in three times a day, noting what actions were skillful and unskillful regarding your labels and attitudes toward others. Check in once in the morning (before noon), once in the afternoon (before 5:00 p.m.), and once in the evening. These should be short notes, allowing you to remember them for your evening review.

MORNING CHECK-IN

Skillful: _____

Unskillful: _____

AFTERNOON CHECK-IN

Skillful: _____

Unskillful: _____

EVENING CHECK-IN

Skillful: _____

Unskillful: _____

EVENING REVIEW

Reflecting on your day, what did you learn?

_____

_____

What was beneficial about this activity?

_____

_____

What was challenging about this activity?

_____

_____

What did you do well today?

_____

_____

How can you make amends for, or improve upon, the unskillful actions of today?

_____

_____

WISDOM EXERCISE THREE, DAY TWO   DATE:

Morning Prayers and/or Reflection

MORNING REFLECTION

- You have a life of recovery filled with support and opportunities. Every day is a new opportunity and fresh start if you choose to take advantage of it.

- Remember that you are not the center of the universe but a valuable part of it. The events that happen in your life, whether you label them good or bad, are all opportunities to grow, learn, and make your life more meaningful.

- Bring to mind people and things you are grateful for. Make them relevant and personal.

- Take some time to reflect on the person you want to be. Set your intention to not waste this day and live it with attention and intention, cultivating the qualities that you find meaningful. Remember, the only thing that separates the person you are from the person you want to be is the action you take. Make a clear and firm commitment to your recovery today. You deserve to live a life free of addiction.

MORNING MEDITATION

Did you do it? _____   How long? _____

Set a clear intention to be aware of how your labels and attitudes toward others affect your interactions with them. See if you can engage with others with an attitude of respect and dignity that includes a vision of their potential.

Check in three times a day, noting what actions were skillful and unskillful regarding your labels and attitudes toward others. Check in once in the morning (before noon), once in the afternoon (before 5:00 p.m.), and once in the evening. These should be short notes, allowing you to remember them for your evening review.

MORNING CHECK-IN

Skillful: _____

Unskillful: _____

AFTERNOON CHECK-IN

Skillful: _____

Unskillful: _____

EVENING CHECK-IN

Skillful: _____

Unskillful: _____

EVENING REVIEW

Reflecting on your day, what did you learn?

_____

_____

What was beneficial about this activity?

_____

_____

What was challenging about this activity?

_____

_____

What did you do well today?

_____

_____

How can you make amends for, or improve upon, the unskillful actions of today?

_____

_____

Wisdom Exercise Four

"Gratitude is not only the greatest of virtues,
but the parent of all others."

MARCUS TULLIUS CICERO

How can we even begin to measure the value of gratitude in our lives? It is not only essential for our recovery but also for finding connection, meaning, and fulfillment in life. When we are grateful, we are not discontent, craving, angry, envious, or worried. Such feelings cannot arise amid gratitude. When we are grateful, we are not looking outside of ourselves for satisfaction. Instead, we are cultivating contentment. There is no clinging, grasping, or projecting. There is fulfillment.

When we are grateful, we recognize the kindnesses and opportunities we have been given and the abundance we already have. We are not watering the seeds of discontent by dwelling on what we don't have. When we reflect upon the opportunities, resources, and abundance we have in our lives—compared with the majority of human beings on Earth, many of whom live without education, electricity, or even basic sustenance—what is it that we are lacking? If we can't learn to be happy with what we have now, what will it take? When we have received so much already and are not happy, what makes us think that getting the next thing or having the next pleasurable experience will somehow quench our thirst for more?

As the quote by Cicero states, gratitude is much more than its own virtue, for its very nature allows us to cultivate more virtuous attitudes and activities. When we take a moment to accurately reflect upon the infinite kindness of all the people who have helped us, most of whom we will never know, a natural state of gratitude arises within us that nurtures and supports our connection to the world and those we share it with. We can take anything we have in our lives—the computer we may be using right now, the phone we are looking at, the clothes we are wearing, the food we enjoy today—and ask, "How many people were involved in its creation and delivery to us?" There is no way to calculate such numbers, since they include those who built the vehicles that transported the items and the roads the vehicles traveled on, those who designed the products, and the people who helped us make a living so we could buy such things. This is just the beginning. As you can see, the list is long!

When we recognize that everything we have in our lives, including our education and opportunities, is the result of innumerable others, not only do we see our good fortune and abundance, but we also find a connection to others. With such a state of gratitude built on our interdependence with all others, it is quite natural that we start engaging with people in more meaningful and virtuous ways.

For the next two days, cultivate gratitude. Again, start your day with a short reflection, noting a few people or things that are truly meaningful to you. Reflect upon all the kindnesses of others that allowed you to have these things or people in your life. As you engage in your day, do your best to maintain an attitude of gratitude, not losing track of all you already have to be grateful for. See how this affects your actions and interactions.

WISDOM EXERCISE FOUR, DAY ONE   **DATE:**

Morning Prayers and/or Reflection

MORNING REFLECTION

- You have a life of recovery filled with support and opportunities. Every day is a new opportunity and fresh start if you choose to take advantage of it.

- Remember that you are not the center of the universe but a valuable part of it. The events that happen in your life, whether you label them good or bad, are all opportunities to grow, learn, and make your life more meaningful.

- Bring to mind people and things you are grateful for. Make them relevant and personal.

- Take some time to reflect on the person you want to be. Set your intention to not waste this day and live it with attention and intention, cultivating the qualities that you find meaningful. Remember, the only thing that separates the person you are from the person you want to be is the action you take. Make a clear and firm commitment to your recovery today. You deserve to live a life free of addiction.

MORNING MEDITATION

Did you do it? _____   How long? _____

Set a clear intention to maintain an attitude of gratitude, not losing track of everything you already have to be grateful for. See how this affects your actions and interactions.

Check in three times a day, noting what actions were skillful and unskillful regarding your attitude of gratitude. Check in once in the morning (before noon), once in the afternoon (before 5:00 p.m.), and once in the evening. These should be short notes, allowing you to remember them for your evening review.

MORNING CHECK-IN

Skillful: _____

Unskillful: _____

AFTERNOON CHECK-IN

Skillful: _____

Unskillful: _____

EVENING CHECK-IN

Skillful: _____

Unskillful: _____

EVENING REVIEW

Reflecting on your day, what did you learn?

_____

_____

What was beneficial about your gratitude practice today?

_____

_____

What was challenging about your gratitude practice today?

_____

_____

What did you do well today?

_____

_____

How can you make amends for, or improve upon, the unskillful actions of today?

_____

_____

WISDOM EXERCISE FOUR, DAY TWO   DATE:

Morning Prayers and/or Reflection

MORNING REFLECTION

- You have a life of recovery filled with support and opportunities. Every day is a new opportunity and fresh start if you choose to take advantage of it.

- Remember that you are not the center of the universe but a valuable part of it. The events that happen in your life, whether you label them good or bad, are all opportunities to grow, learn, and make your life more meaningful.

- Bring to mind people and things you are grateful for. Make them relevant and personal.

- Take some time to reflect on the person you want to be. Set your intention to not waste this day and live it with attention and intention, cultivating the qualities that you find meaningful. Remember, the only thing that separates the person you are from the person you want to be is the action you take. Make a clear and firm commitment to your recovery today. You deserve to live a life free of addiction.

MORNING MEDITATION

Did you do it? _____   How long? _____

Set a clear intention to maintain an attitude of gratitude, not losing track of everything you already have to be grateful for. See how this affects your actions and interactions.

Check in three times a day, noting what actions were skillful and unskillful regarding your attitude of gratitude. Check in once in the morning (before noon), once in the afternoon (before 5:00 p.m.), and once in the evening. These should be short notes, allowing you to remember them for your evening review.

MORNING CHECK-IN

Skillful: _____

Unskillful: _____

AFTERNOON CHECK-IN

Skillful: _____

Unskillful: _____

EVENING CHECK-IN

Skillful: _____

Unskillful: _____

EVENING REVIEW

Reflecting on your day, what did you learn?

_____

_____

What was beneficial about your gratitude practice today?

_____

_____

What was challenging about your gratitude practice today?

_____

_____

What did you do well today?

_____

_____

How can you make amends for, or improve upon, the unskillful actions of today?

_____

_____

Wisdom Exercise Five

"Don't let yesterday use up too much of today."

CHEROKEE PROVERB

Though we may know it intellectually, it is truly a practice to realize that yesterday no longer exists. It is true our past has created our present, and our past has shaped us. We could not be who we are today without all the experiences we have had, whether they were joyful, educational, tragic, or somewhere in between. However, our past need not dictate our future, nor, as the Cherokee proverb reminds us, prevent us from fully living today.

For us to fully grow in our recovery, it is important to remember that, while we cannot change the past, we can learn from it. Our past can be a valuable resource, helping us learn from our experiences and fully develop our potential. Unfortunately, instead of using the past as a valuable resource, we often fall victim to it. We tend to carry the regrets and wounds of yesterday with us, keeping them alive long after the actual events have faded into history. In doing so, we do not allow them to heal and continue to feel their pain.

It is much more helpful to let go of resentments, regrets, and old emotional pain related to the past. Instead of focusing on past pain, we can focus on the inner resources and resiliency we have developed as a result of the pain, as well as the lessons we have learned from going through it.

Life offers us lessons and opportunities to fully develop our highest potential. Sometimes the lessons are difficult, and sometimes they are easy. Though we always want the easy ones, the challenging lessons tend to allow us to grow the most.

Today recognize this day as the first day of the rest of your life and the past does not need to dictate your future. When regrets or old wounds start to occupy your attention, recall how you have grown and let them go. Bring your attention back to today and remember that the only thing that separates the person you are from the person you want to be is the action you take.

WISDOM EXERCISE FIVE, DAY ONE   DATE:

Morning Prayers and/or Reflection

MORNING REFLECTION

- You have a life of recovery filled with support and opportunities. Every day is a new opportunity and fresh start if you choose to take advantage of it.

- Remember that you are not the center of the universe but a valuable part of it. The events that happen in your life, whether you label them good or bad, are all opportunities to grow, learn, and make your life more meaningful.

- Bring to mind people and things you are grateful for. Make them relevant and personal.

- Take some time to reflect on the person you want to be. Set your intention to not waste this day and live it with attention and intention, cultivating the qualities that you find meaningful. Remember, the only thing that separates the person you are from the person you want to be is the action you take. Make a clear and firm commitment to your recovery today. You deserve to live a life free of addiction.

MORNING MEDITATION

Did you do it? _____   How long? _____

Set a clear intention to maintain an attitude of gratitude, not losing track of everything you already have to be grateful for. See how this affects your actions and interactions.

Check in three times a day, noting what actions were skillful and unskillful regarding your attitude of gratitude. Check in once in the morning (before noon), once in the afternoon (before 5:00 p.m.), and once in the evening. These should be short notes, allowing you to remember them for your evening review.

MORNING CHECK-IN

Skillful: _____

Unskillful: _____

AFTERNOON CHECK-IN

Skillful: _____

Unskillful: _____

EVENING CHECK-IN

Skillful: _____

Unskillful: _____

EVENING REVIEW

Reflecting on your day, what did you learn?

_____

_____

What was beneficial about your gratitude practice today?

_____

_____

What was challenging about your gratitude practice today?

_____

_____

What did you do well today?

_____

_____

How can you make amends for, or improve upon, the unskillful actions of today?

_____

_____

WISDOM REVIEW

What were the most valuable lessons you learned this week?

_____

_____

_____

What wisdom did you discover this week that you would like to continue to develop?

_____

_____

_____

What did you do well this week that supports your recovery?

_____

_____

_____

MINDFULNESS SKILLS
SUMMARY AND REVIEW

As you have engaged in your mindfulness practice to this point, you have had the opportunity to work on developing a routine that allows you to start your day consciously with attention and intention, check in on your intentions and actions throughout the day, and review your day in the evening so you can identify what you are doing well and where you can improve. This is an incredibly powerful habit to cultivate, one that is foundational to transforming your life in the ways you find most meaningful. If you are still struggling for consistency, that is completely normal. You are in the process of creating a new habit and it takes time. Be easy on yourself and remember every day is a new opportunity.

You have also had some experience developing a meditation practice. Meditation is the direct antidote to one of the most significant barriers preventing people from making healthy choices that support their recovery and values: an obsessive, compulsive, and distracted mind. Having a consistent meditation practice is the key that unlocks the door to living mindfully. It empowers you to develop your attention, no longer powerless over every thought, impulse, or worry that arises, and allows space to make choices that are conducive to the life you want to live.

In your practice, you have explored and identified your values, noting and contrasting the effects of engaging in actions that are in alignment with them and those that are not. The value exercises provide you the opportunity to directly realize a fundamental truth: your well-being, sense of value and worthiness, as well as your genuine happiness, is directly related to living in alignment with your values and doing things that are meaningful. To put it simply, lasting happiness comes from doing things you feel good about, not from doing things that make you feel good. Such a realization is the path back to sanity as you choose attitudes, actions, and habits that actually support the person you want to be instead of things that lead to feelings of shame and regret.

Living mindfully, with attention and intention, allows you to gain wisdom and insight regarding the subjective experience of life, your belief system, the world you live in, and your relationship to it. An enormous amount of suffering in life stems from our own self-centered thinking and a basic misunderstanding of how life works. You have a chance to step out of self-centered thinking, remembering that life is actually messy for everyone. No one is immune from accidents, relationship issues, sickness, health problems, emotional pain, or the ups and downs of the economy. Cultivating wise acceptance enables you to skillfully engage with life on life's terms, learning to meet the challenges that will inevitably arise and turn them into opportunities to grow.

Mindfulness also empowers you to discover the influence your attitudes have on how you experience people, events, and yourself. As you shift or change your attitude, your experience of people and events changes. Your practice of intentionally cultivating healthy attitudes of equanimity, loving-kindness, and compassion provides a clear insight into its transformative power. You have the ability to counteract harmful attitudes with productive ones and alter your experience by changing your attitude or perspective of it.

Essentially, the tools of Mindfulness in Recovery are designed to help you be mindful of the source of the majority of your mental and emotional suffering—engaging in actions that are contrary to your deepest values—as well as the source of your genuine happiness—engaging in actions that support your deepest values.

This process, consistently practiced, not only liberates you from your addictions but also the unhealthy and senseless habits, attitudes, and thoughts that prevent you from recognizing your own worthiness and value as a human being. Living mindfully in recovery, you will find a new freedom, the freedom to actively engage in your life wisely, skillfully embracing life on life's terms as you become the person you want to be in a life you find meaningful.

Now look back over the lessons you have learned and bring some clarity to them through this next series of questions.

1. List three values that are most important to you at this time.

   a. _____

   b. _____

   c. _____

2. Describe attitudes, habits, and actions that support your values and the person you want to be.

_____

_____

_____

_____

_____

3. Describe attitudes, habits, and actions that you are prone to that counter your values and the person you want to be.

_____

_____

_____

_____

_____

4. What are you doing well?

_____

_____

_____

5. What would you like to improve upon?

_____

_____

_____

6. What would you like to explore more?

_____

_____

_____

Self-Directed Daily Mindfulness

Explore a week of self-directed daily mindfulness activities. Look back over the past exercises and find some that you would like to investigate more deeply. Be sure to fill out each daily activity the night before you are to begin, so you are clear on your intention as soon as you wake up.

SELF-DIRECTED MINDFULNESS DAY ONE   DATE:

Morning Prayers and/or Reflection

MORNING REFLECTION

- You have a life of recovery filled with support and opportunities. Every day is a new opportunity and fresh start if you choose to take advantage of it.

- Remember that you are not the center of the universe but a valuable part of it. The events that happen in your life, whether you label them good or bad, are all opportunities to grow, learn, and make your life more meaningful.

- Bring to mind people and things you are grateful for. Make them relevant and personal.

- Take some time to reflect on the person you want to be. Set your intention to not waste this day and live it with attention and intention, cultivating the qualities that you find meaningful. Remember, the only thing that separates the person you are from the person you want to be is the action you take. Make a clear and firm commitment to your recovery today. You deserve to live a life free of addiction.

MORNING MEDITATION

Did you do it? _____ How long? _____

Set a clear intention for the day.

_____

_____

Check in three times a day, noting what actions were skillful and unskillful regarding your attitude of gratitude. Check in once in the morning (before noon), once in the afternoon (before 5:00 p.m.), and once in the evening. These should be short notes, allowing you to remember them for your evening review.

MORNING CHECK-IN

Skillful: _____

Unskillful: _____

AFTERNOON CHECK-IN

Skillful: _____

Unskillful: _____

EVENING CHECK-IN

Skillful: _____

Unskillful: _____

EVENING REVIEW

Reflecting on your day, what did you learn?

_____

_____

What was beneficial about your practice today?

_____

_____

What was challenging about your practice today?

_____

_____

What did you do well today?

_____

_____

How can you make amends for, or improve upon, the unskillful actions of today?

_____

_____

SELF-DIRECTED MINDFULNESS DAY TWO   DATE:

Morning Prayers and/or Reflection

MORNING REFLECTION

- You have a life of recovery filled with support and opportunities. Every day is a new opportunity and fresh start if you choose to take advantage of it.

- Remember that you are not the center of the universe but a valuable part of it. The events that happen in your life, whether you label them good or bad, are all opportunities to grow, learn, and make your life more meaningful.

- Bring to mind people and things you are grateful for. Make them relevant and personal.

- Take some time to reflect on the person you want to be. Set your intention to not waste this day and live it with attention and intention, cultivating the qualities that you find meaningful. Remember, the only thing that separates the person you are from the person you want to be is the action you take. Make a clear and firm commitment to your recovery today. You deserve to live a life free of addiction.

MORNING MEDITATION

Did you do it? _____   How long? _____

Set a clear intention for the day.

_____

_____

Check in three times a day, noting what actions were skillful and unskillful regarding your attitude of gratitude. Check in once in the morning (before noon), once in the afternoon (before 5:00 p.m.), and once in the evening. These should be short notes, allowing you to remember them for your evening review.

MORNING CHECK-IN

Skillful: _____

Unskillful: _____

AFTERNOON CHECK-IN

Skillful: _____

Unskillful: _____

EVENING CHECK-IN

Skillful: _____

Unskillful: _____

EVENING REVIEW

Reflecting on your day, what did you learn?

_____

_____

What was beneficial about your practice today?

_____

_____

What was challenging about your practice today?

_____

_____

What did you do well today?

_____

_____

How can you make amends for, or improve upon, the unskillful actions of today?

_____

_____

SELF-DIRECTED MINDFULNESS DAY THREE   DATE:

Morning Prayers and/or Reflection

MORNING REFLECTION

- You have a life of recovery filled with support and opportunities. Every day is a new opportunity and fresh start if you choose to take advantage of it.

- Remember that you are not the center of the universe but a valuable part of it. The events that happen in your life, whether you label them good or bad, are all opportunities to grow, learn, and make your life more meaningful.

- Bring to mind people and things you are grateful for. Make them relevant and personal.

- Take some time to reflect on the person you want to be. Set your intention to not waste this day and live it with attention and intention, cultivating the qualities that you find meaningful. Remember, the only thing that separates the person you are from the person you want to be is the action you take. Make a clear and firm commitment to your recovery today. You deserve to live a life free of addiction.

MORNING MEDITATION

Did you do it? _____   How long? _____

Set a clear intention for the day.

_____

_____

Check in three times a day, noting what actions were skillful and unskillful regarding your attitude of gratitude. Check in once in the morning (before noon), once in the afternoon (before 5:00 p.m.), and once in the evening. These should be short notes, allowing you to remember them for your evening review.

MORNING CHECK-IN

Skillful: _____

Unskillful: _____

AFTERNOON CHECK-IN

Skillful: _____

Unskillful: _____

EVENING CHECK-IN

Skillful: _____

Unskillful: _____

EVENING REVIEW

Reflecting on your day, what did you learn?

_____

_____

What was beneficial about your practice today?

_____

_____

What was challenging about your practice today?

_____

_____

What did you do well today?

_____

_____

How can you make amends for, or improve upon, the unskillful actions of today?

_____

_____

SELF-DIRECTED MINDFULNESS DAY FOUR   DATE:

Morning Prayers and/or Reflection

MORNING REFLECTION

- You have a life of recovery filled with support and opportunities. Every day is a new opportunity and fresh start if you choose to take advantage of it.

- Remember that you are not the center of the universe but a valuable part of it. The events that happen in your life, whether you label them good or bad, are all opportunities to grow, learn, and make your life more meaningful.

- Bring to mind people and things you are grateful for. Make them relevant and personal.

- Take some time to reflect on the person you want to be. Set your intention to not waste this day and live it with attention and intention, cultivating the qualities that you find meaningful. Remember, the only thing that separates the person you are from the person you want to be is the action you take. Make a clear and firm commitment to your recovery today. You deserve to live a life free of addiction.

MORNING MEDITATION

Did you do it? _____   How long? _____

Set a clear intention for the day.

_____

_____

Check in three times a day, noting what actions were skillful and unskillful regarding your attitude of gratitude. Check in once in the morning (before noon), once in the afternoon (before 5:00 p.m.), and once in the evening. These should be short notes, allowing you to remember them for your evening review.

MORNING CHECK-IN

Skillful: _____

Unskillful: _____

AFTERNOON CHECK-IN

Skillful: _____

Unskillful: _____

EVENING CHECK-IN

Skillful: _____

Unskillful: _____

EVENING REVIEW

Reflecting on your day, what did you learn?

_____

_____

What was beneficial about your practice today?

_____

_____

What was challenging about your practice today?

_____

_____

What did you do well today?

_____

_____

How can you make amends for, or improve upon, the unskillful actions of today?

_____

_____

SELF-DIRECTED MINDFULNESS DAY FIVE   DATE:

Morning Prayers and/or Reflection

MORNING REFLECTION

- You have a life of recovery filled with support and opportunities. Every day is a new opportunity and fresh start if you choose to take advantage of it.

- Remember that you are not the center of the universe but a valuable part of it. The events that happen in your life, whether you label them good or bad, are all opportunities to grow, learn, and make your life more meaningful.

- Bring to mind people and things you are grateful for. Make them relevant and personal.

- Take some time to reflect on the person you want to be. Set your intention to not waste this day and live it with attention and intention, cultivating the qualities that you find meaningful. Remember, the only thing that separates the person you are from the person you want to be is the action you take. Make a clear and firm commitment to your recovery today. You deserve to live a life free of addiction.

MORNING MEDITATION

Did you do it? _____   How long? _____

Set a clear intention for the day.

_____

_____

Check in three times a day, noting what actions were skillful and unskillful regarding your attitude of gratitude. Check in once in the morning (before noon), once in the afternoon (before 5:00 p.m.), and once in the evening. These should be short notes, allowing you to remember them for your evening review.

MORNING CHECK-IN

Skillful: _____

Unskillful: _____

AFTERNOON CHECK-IN

Skillful: _____

Unskillful: _____

EVENING CHECK-IN

Skillful: _____

Unskillful: _____

EVENING REVIEW

Reflecting on your day, what did you learn?

_____

_____

What was beneficial about your practice today?

_____

_____

What was challenging about your practice today?

_____

_____

What did you do well today?

_____

_____

How can you make amends for, or improve upon, the unskillful actions of today?

_____

_____

SELF-DIRECTED MINDFULNESS DAY SIX   DATE:

Morning Prayers and/or Reflection

MORNING REFLECTION

- You have a life of recovery filled with support and opportunities. Every day is a new opportunity and fresh start if you choose to take advantage of it.

- Remember that you are not the center of the universe but a valuable part of it. The events that happen in your life, whether you label them good or bad, are all opportunities to grow, learn, and make your life more meaningful.

- Bring to mind people and things you are grateful for. Make them relevant and personal.

- Take some time to reflect on the person you want to be. Set your intention to not waste this day and live it with attention and intention, cultivating the qualities that you find meaningful. Remember, the only thing that separates the person you are from the person you want to be is the action you take. Make a clear and firm commitment to your recovery today. You deserve to live a life free of addiction.

MORNING MEDITATION

Did you do it? _____   How long? _____

Set a clear intention for the day.

_____

_____

Check in three times a day, noting what actions were skillful and unskillful regarding your attitude of gratitude. Check in once in the morning (before noon), once in the afternoon (before 5:00 p.m.), and once in the evening. These should be short notes, allowing you to remember them for your evening review.

MORNING CHECK-IN

Skillful: _____

Unskillful: _____

AFTERNOON CHECK-IN

Skillful: _____

Unskillful: _____

EVENING CHECK-IN

Skillful: _____

Unskillful: _____

EVENING REVIEW

Reflecting on your day, what did you learn?

_____

_____

What was beneficial about your practice today?

_____

_____

What was challenging about your practice today?

_____

_____

What did you do well today?

_____

_____

How can you make amends for, or improve upon, the unskillful actions of today?

_____

_____

SELF-DIRECTED MINDFULNESS DAY SEVEN   DATE:

Morning Prayers and/or Reflection

MORNING REFLECTION

- You have a life of recovery filled with support and opportunities. Every day is a new opportunity and fresh start if you choose to take advantage of it.

- Remember that you are not the center of the universe but a valuable part of it. The events that happen in your life, whether you label them good or bad, are all opportunities to grow, learn, and make your life more meaningful.

- Bring to mind people and things you are grateful for. Make them relevant and personal.

- Take some time to reflect on the person you want to be. Set your intention to not waste this day and live it with attention and intention, cultivating the qualities that you find meaningful. Remember, the only thing that separates the person you are from the person you want to be is the action you take. Make a clear and firm commitment to your recovery today. You deserve to live a life free of addiction.

MORNING MEDITATION

Did you do it? _____ How long? _____

Set a clear intention for the day.

_____

_____

Check in three times a day, noting what actions were skillful and unskillful regarding your attitude of gratitude. Check in once in the morning (before noon), once in the afternoon (before 5:00 p.m.), and once in the evening. These should be short notes, allowing you to remember them for your evening review.

MORNING CHECK-IN

Skillful: _____

Unskillful: _____

AFTERNOON CHECK-IN

Skillful: _____

Unskillful: _____

EVENING CHECK-IN

Skillful: _____

Unskillful: _____

EVENING REVIEW

Reflecting on your day, what did you learn?

_____

_____

What was beneficial about your practice today?

_____

_____

What was challenging about your practice today?

_____

_____

What did you do well today?

_____

_____

How can you make amends for, or improve upon, the unskillful actions of today?

_____

_____

WEEKLY REVIEW

What were the most valuable lessons you learned this week?

_____

_____

_____

What wisdom did you discover this week that you would like to continue to develop?

_____

_____

_____

What did you do well this week that supports your recovery?

_____

_____

_____

What would you like to improve upon?

_____

_____

_____

CONTINUING THE PRACTICE

Mindfulness is a practice. As with any other practice, the more you do it the better results you will have. I hope that you have already found tremendous benefit and have had at least a glimpse of the freedom and fulfillment that is possible in your recovery.

Do your best to maintain a daily practice and actively utilize any and all of the tools you have found useful. The Mindfulness in Recovery community is a valuable resource to support you as you continue your practice. It provides daily support, inspiration, lessons, and activities, as well as a community of other members dedicated to living life fully in recovery. You can learn more online at www.mindfulnessinrecovery.org.

Helpful Advice to Remember

Habits grow weaker or stronger in relation to repetition. You can change them consciously. As Aristotle put it, "We are what we repeatedly do. Excellence, then, is not an act, but a habit."

Surround yourself as much as possible with people and environments that are supportive to your recovery. As the old saying goes, "if you hang around the barber shop long enough, you are going to get a haircut."

Be gentle with yourself, there is nothing beneficial about beating yourself up or comparing yourself with some ideal of who you think you ought to be. It is more accurate and productive to compare yourself with who you used to be and note the progress you have made.

Mistakes are a natural and unavoidable part of life for everyone. They always provide you with invaluable lessons to become a better person.

You do not need to wait for some ideal time to improve. Every moment, every breath, is a new opportunity. An opportunity to let go of the past and become the person you choose to be.

Patience is an action and a skill to be cultivated. It actually solves more problems that most other actions.

ABOUT MINDFULNESS IN RECOVERY

Mindfulness in Recovery's primary mission is to provide our members with skills, activities, and a supportive community to cultivate mindfulness in their daily lives, empowering them to make healthy choices in alignment with their personal values and beliefs so they can live meaningful lives in recovery.

Mindfulness in Recovery was designed to support members of all faiths and spiritual traditions, as well as those without a spiritual tradition. We do not promote any particular faith or belief system. It is our firm conviction that everyone—regardless of race, religion, gender, or orientation—deserves to live a meaningful and happy life in recovery. It is our belief that this is best accomplished when people have the resources and tools to live the lives they find meaningful with attention and intention—lives that are in alignment with their own values and allow them to flourish.

VALUES LIST

Acceptance	Compassion	Duty
Accomplishment	Competence	Ease
Accountability	Competitiveness	Effectiveness
Achievement	Concentration	Empathy
Acknowledgment	Confidence	Enjoyment
Activism	Conformity	Enthusiasm
Adaptability	Connection	Equality
Adventure	Consciousness	Ethics
Altruism	Consistency	Fairness
Ambition	Contentment	Faith
Appreciation	Continuous Improvement	Family
Assertiveness	Conviction	Fearlessness
Attentiveness	Cooperation	Fidelity
Awareness	Courage	Freedom
Balance	Courtesy	Friendliness
Beauty	Creativity	Fun
Being the best	Credibility	Generosity
Belonging	Curiosity	Goodness
Benevolence	Decisiveness	Grace
Bravery	Democracy	Gratitude
Calmness	Dependability	Growth
Camaraderie	Determination	Happiness
Candor	Devotion	Hard Work
Care	Dignity	Helpfulness
Charity	Diligence	Holiness
Cheerfulness	Discipline	Honesty
Comfort	Discretion	Hopefulness
Commitment	Diversity	Humility
Community	Drive	Humor

VALUES LIST (CONTINUED)

Impartiality

Inclusiveness

Independence

Individuality

Inner Harmony

Inquisitiveness

Insightfulness

Integrity

Intelligence

Intimacy

Introspection

Intuitiveness

Joy

Justice

Kindness

Leadership

Legacy

Love

Loyalty

Making a Difference

Merit

Mindfulness

Motivation

Non-conformity

Obedience

Open-mindedness

Optimism

Order

Originality

Passion

Patience

Peacefulness

Perseverance

Playfulness

Power

Prudence

Punctuality

Quality-orientation

Rationality

Reasonableness

Relaxation

Reliability

Reputation

Resilience

Resolve

Resourcefulness

Respect

Responsibility

Restraint

Results-oriented

Reverence

Self-actualization

Self-respect

Selflessness

Sensitivity

Serenity

Service

Sharing

Simplicity

Sincerity

Skillfulness

Spontaneity

Stability

Status

Stillness

Success

Teamwork

Temperance

Thoroughness

Thoughtfulness

Tolerance

Traditionalism

Trustworthiness

Truth

Uniqueness

Usefulness

Virtue

Vitality

Willingness

Wisdom

Wonder

Worthiness

DAILY MORNING REFLECTIONS

*You have a life of recovery filled with
support and opportunities. Every day
is a new opportunity and fresh start if
you choose to take advantage of it.*

FIRST REFLECTION

*Remember that you are not the center of
the universe but a valuable part of it.
The events that happen in your life, whether you
label them good or bad, are all opportunities to grow,
learn, and make your life more meaningful.*

SECOND REFLECTION

*Bring to mind people and things you are grateful for.
Make them relevant and personal.*

THIRD REFLECTION

*Take some time to reflect on the person you want to be. Set your
intention to not waste this day and live it with attention and
intention, cultivating the qualities that you find meaningful.
Remember, the only thing that separates the person you are
from the person you want to be is the action you take.
Make a clear and firm commitment to your recovery today.
You deserve to live a life free of addiction.*

FOURTH REFLECTION

Printed in the USA
CPSIA information can be obtained
at www.ICGtesting.com
JSHW060040150824
68134JS00028B/2575

9 781942 094852